ART FROM THE HEART

POEMS BY

ERIC LEVINE

Art from the Heart
Copyright © 2018 By Eric Levine

ISBN-13: 978-1544201719

ISBN-10: 1544201710

For my parents: Thank you for always encouraging me, and believing in everything that I do

Contents

Acknowledgements

I would to thank everyone who helped make this book possible.

Thank you to my family: Mom, Stephanie, Dan, Bruce, Ron, and Debbie for listening to and reading my poems, and for your valuable feedback. It was much appreciated.

To the kids: Melissa, Rachel, Shira, and Marni thank you also for your encouragement and support. I know you will be successful in everything that you do. You guys rock.

To my friends: Mike and Heather, Steve and Susan, Yolanda and Saul, Jonathan and Lauren, Rick and Ellie, and brothers Dave and Nathan thank you so much for your friendship and advice. Pam, thank you again for reading my book and for your corrections they were very helpful.

To the Cardozo men and women's health, physical education, and dance teachers, and support staff: Thank you for your encouragement it was very much appreciated. Thank you also for being great co-workers, and for all the laughs we shared. It made my teaching career truly enjoyable.

Chapter 1: God and the Holy Land

A Walk with the Prophets

I put on my sandals as centuries ago,
And enter the night with no expectations to show.
Zion seems like a memory to me.

Ghosts pass by me and wave,
The lights of Jerusalem are in the distance,
As is Herzl's grave.

I walk the paths of prophets tonight.
Battles and triumphs,
Song and dance,
Wandering this planet, alone in a trance.

And then finally back
To where we were before,
Homeward to Jerusalem,
Zion restored.
Asleep with the prophets,
A wanderer no more.

Dawn over Auschwitz

Dawn broke over Auschwitz, and all I could do was stare.
Dawn broke over Auschwitz, and all I could do was stare.

I went with my mother to get milk, and pretended that it wasn't there.
I went with my father for the paper, and pretended that it wasn't there,

But the trains kept coming and coming, and no one seemed to care.
The trains unloaded their cargo, but no one seemed to care.

I smelled the smoke at night as it wafted in the air.
I try to sleep at night, but their cries are in the air.

I see them in my dreams sometimes when I can get some sleep,
They are constantly calling me, and I always hear them plead.

And now that I am an adult and have my own children too,
I want to tell them what we did,
What horrible things to the Jews.

My precious gift it's really unfair,
That dawn broke over Auschwitz and no one seemed to care,
And that I was witness, and all I did was stare.

Elijah About Town

If Elijah were to walk about my town during Passover he would feel
the candle like warmth of families.
If he peered into windows he would see our smiling faces,
The young, the old, all joined together as one.
Smiles,
Singing,
And joy.
Drinking several cups of wine.
More joy times four,
And don't forget the laughter of a mispronounced Haggadah reading.
The silliness,
"The Egyptians made us supper,"
"Moses, hold my rod!"
"Rabbi Jose had a few tacos instead of Matzah."
People might grumble because they are getting hungry,
Sometimes we are somber especially when there is a missing seat that
held a loved one,
But every year there are more joyous memories created, and
sometimes some new babies.
Oh God,
Thank you.
It is enough for me.

God Can You Hear Me?

God is dead,
That's what John Lennon said,
And I truly thought the same thing,
Until one night
On a porch with rain like a herd of bison running across the plains,
Under a metal awning,
I found God.
I felt God.
He was alive and mad,
But mad at no one in particular.
I felt fear from his thunder, and awe-inspiring lightning,
I realized that the word of God could be heard inside and outside,
But for me, I seek strength and courage from my peers.
We sing his praises, but we should shout them too because
In each of us lies God.
We search for meaning, recognition, and purpose.
God is our tour guide, butler, light bulb, and none of these things,
But, if we look inside ourselves,
Peel away the layers until we reach our soul, we may find a golden drop of rain,
A child is waiting to be born,
We know who our father is, but it is up to God to
Steer him on his path, and let him choose his destiny.
Are you ready to begin?
Put your trust in God and believe in yourself, and anything is possible.

Going, Going, God

I met a man the other day, but he didn't know who he was,
I thought amnesia had sent in, but he just wasn't religious.

Oh, Cohen, oh Levite, oh Israelite, oh Meyer, why have
You allowed your religion to disappear?

When trouble hits we run for cover,
We run for our families, or we run for our lovers.

We grab our children, and call the doctor,
But only turn to God when it all seems over.

You see God is with us every day,
He watches our progress, and listens to what we say.

He's there for us to Atlas our burden,
He wants the best for all his children.

God means courage, calm, and peace of mind,
When he's with me I don' t ever feel left behind.

So give God a call every once in a while,
Or even better do it often, and you'll likely smile.

Cause luck is not luck anymore today,
It's the deeds we do, and the truths we say.

It's keeping the flame of courage inside,
It's being proud of our culture, and proud to be alive.

It's saying, " I'm Jewish or another religion, and I believe in God,"
And I stand here knowing who I am, and the path that I trod.

Israel

Oh Israel, show me your beautiful light.
Hills surround you with tranquility,
And a feeling of love permeates the air.
God's chosen people to befriend the land, and redeem it.
The Garden of Eden is lost somewhere,
But I know where you are,
Oh oasis in a mass of swirling desert sands,
Oh gem, oh treasure, reveal yourself so all may partake and taste your
sweetness.
Israel with many a clime, and many a populace,
A veritable smorgasbord of wonderful things to see and explore,
To experience is to know,
To know is to grow,
And to grow in Israel in any way is to be content.

Left out of the Book of Life

I screwed her,
I cursed them,
And said to God "Piss off!"
And then when my time came I was truly worse off.

On my deathbed God came with a spear of fire and a measuring stand,
He asked me once more if I would repent,
And if I wanted to be a new man.

But I did not understand what repentance meant or what it was for,
And I awoke beside the river Styx, and cannot change my choices
anymore.

I turn the horrible wheel endlessly and push the stone uphill,
My wine jugs all always empty, and can never be filled.

Once a year, a holiday comes to teach man to forgive,
Once a year we ask God, "I'm sorry will you let me live?"
And on that day we fast and thirst to remember who we are, and what
we did.

We beat our breasts, chant, and moan,
In the temple we are together, but in the end we are all alone.

Though our parents made us, God is the spark,
And so I say it's never too late or too far,
To remember what you said, what you did, and most importantly who
you are.

Olive Tree

I used to be on my own,
Until I found my true home.

A place where we can grow,
A place I'm sure you know.

I have green in my bones,
And live by many homes.

I helped transform the land
And make it lush and green,
I helped make Israel even more beautiful than it's been.

This holiday remember what gifts I bestow and try to savor me,
When you taste my sweetness remember the land by the sea.

Peace When?

Leah Rabin shed a tear at her husband's grave,
It landed on the ground, and soon others came.

The water started flowing the ground began to thunder,
The footsteps of the mourners, and cries of shock and wonder.

The flowers started piling,
The rocks grew wide and tall,
The people kept coming,
Till there was no space at all.

The kaddish said in union,
The lamentations for Rabin,
Who gave his life for peace,
But what does it all mean?

We'll remember his sacrifice,
And the lives that he touched,
Peace will come yet in the Middle East,
If only we can trust.

Song of Rain on Yom Kippur in Temple Israel

The rumblings began on Friday night,
I closed my eyes to ease my fright.

It went on and on for nearly an hour,
And then I listened to the storm's great power.

A drop of rain, and then another,
A page turned, tears were collected like brothers.

My heart beat steadily, and the rain continued,
The thunder would go on, and yelled on occasion.

Thunder in need of fulfillment, or simply just a change,
The lightning was evident, and echoed with the sound of rage.

The rain became a monsoon, when I listened with intent,
And then there was silence, because the Rabbi was content.

Although in my heart I was still unsure,
But clearly the world outside was quite verdure.

As I walked away, and fasted the next week,
I thought of shofars, and the courage that I seek,
I thought of God, and am no longer meek.

S.O.S. to God

S.O.S. to God,
Why am I here?
Why was I brought into this world?
I am a star among the multitude,
A grain of sand on the beach,
A speck of dust out west.

S.O.S. to God,
Help me, and show me the way,
I think therefore I'm unsure,
Feelings of doubt wash over me,
So many possibilities nothing set in stone,
Why do I feel so alone?

S.O.S. to God,
In a crowded room I am a stranger,
The sun rises, people are happy, and so many cry,
I wish for greatness,
I don't want descent,
I want happiness,
I don't want to relent,
I committed no sins, and have no need to repent.

S.O.S. to God,
I have feelings to vent.

Toils and hardships I feel swamped by them all,
Trying to escape to where I can't fail or fall,
Biblical signs are uncommon,
No Moses of late,
Just shamans and fakers, and no one first rate,

S.O.S. to God,
Just what is my fate?

The Eternal Lights

The buttons are not fiery,
They cast a pale orange glow,
Many times you pass them without thinking about them,
Most of the time they are not noticed at all.
The names are remembered by some, and unknown to others,
But I remember him as warm, gentle, and kind,
When I saw his light it brought back a flood of memories,
I was sad and then happy, and back again.
His spirit was not reduced to a name on the wall of memory,
No, like the state of Israel, he was light among the nations of people.
Then, when a two year old came, and tried to extinguish his light,
I was tempted to scold the child,
But the young are simply reminders of new replacing old.
So instead of yelling I pointed to an empty plaque,
You have your life ahead I said,
Make something good of it,
Make others lives better for it,
Start today, you've been told.

Chapter 2: Peace

A Girl Seven Years Old, Living in Syria

Each day I watch the bombs fall down on our house, and on our street,
Each day I pray for them to end, and a little more for us to eat.

I don't understand why the parents of the children can't get along,
I don't understand why they give each other bombs, instead of simply
love or sing them songs.

I went to school a long time ago, but my school isn't here, and my
teacher was told to go.

I miss my friends, my dog, and the quiet of the night,
I miss being comfortable, and dislike always feeling fright,
I hope someday things will be all right,
I hope someday somebody will learn of our plight.

I'll send this message by pigeon, or through prayers to God,
Whoever hears it please come quickly as I'm out of paper, and nearly
out of light.

Dublane

There are dirges being sung in Dublane,
I heard them on the news the other day.

The gymnasiums are clean and new,
The children are visibly shaken, but back at school.

I remember vaguely the maelstrom, but it's so far away I can't
understand.
I've heard the stories of the gunman crazy shooting spell,
And children dying with little chance of life to tell.

What they saw in his face,
No last goodbyes, or "Love you's" to say.
There are dirges being sung in Dublane today,
But I am here in New York, so I will light a candle, and simply pray.

Freedom in Burma

Freedom!
I was in Myanmar just trying to bring peace,
When you saw me with the leaflets as I tried to leave.

But you stopped me, and said I couldn't go,
I screamed and screamed to let me go.

But you arrested me, and put me in jail,
I didn't have a phone call,
Or any chance of bail.

The trial was speedy,
But my lawyer didn't show,
It wasn't a fee he wanted,
He was just an unknown.

In a land of dictators, famines, and drugs,
Hunger season, beatings, and God help me plenty of thugs.

And just when you thought you might help things improve,
I read of your plight in the daily news.

And saw you demonstrate,
You tried to run away,
I called the president, but he didn't answer, or just couldn't say,
Why peace is so fragile,
In so many ways.

Other countries cry,
Other girls cry,
They cry "Freedom!"

Freedom, freedom, freedom.
Freedom,
Ah, but just tell me when?

Hate

Anti-Semitic remarks permeate the air,
Bitter words about Jews she doesn't care.

Callous, unthinking, are they devils or what?
Do you think they have horns, and really sell smut?

Every one of them is bearded and venal,
Friends they are not, but only evil.

Grating is to hear her say this,
Hebrews have brought the world much bliss.

Imagine such stereotypes today,
Just hearing her hurts me in a big way.

Knowing that what she says isn't true,
Listening just makes me feel blue.

Ma'am please stop you don't know the facts.
Only by keeping your mind open,
Prevents you from evil words spoken.

Quietly listening to others,
Represents the way to become true brothers.

So I ask you at this time,
To understand this rhyme.

U can do it if you really want to,
Veritas, it's true.

We all can live in peace.
Xcept if we live our lives filled with hate,
You wouldn't want that to be your fate.

Zion and it's message are applicable to all,
Lets work together we'll have a ball.

I Wish I Could Just Travel

I wish I could just travel, and see the world each week,
I wish I could just travel, and avoid being meek.

I would gaze at the fish beneath the sea,
I would climb mountains, and breathe the clean air of trees,
I would take time to just be me,
I would take time to enjoy being free.

I would take trains to faraway lands,
I would forgo Google translate, and learn the language of the local man.

I would finally be complete, and my heart would certainly soar,
Hang glide or bungee jump? What else could you ask for?

An African safari?
A rain forest breeze?
The animals of the world,
Cry out for their needs,
The natives cry, but not for me.

Poverty speaks though their ancient stones are silent,
Pyramids of Egypt wait for me to explore, and to find them.

I wish I had the time or job that gave me the chance,
To take some risks, and finally advance.

All I have is me, and that is a lot,
I do have family and friends that care, but too often dream not.

They give me love, and usually take my side,
If could only I could make some progress, and make my dreams come alive.

I Wish I Knew My Father

I wish I knew my father,
Knew him for who he is,
I wish we had gone to more ball games,
And wish that we were friends.

I wish I could turn to him, and he would sympathize,
But often there is coldness in his beautiful hazel eyes.

He tries to kiss me, and I turn away,
I know I should reciprocate, but it often seems too late.

He tells you stories at dinner when pressed to reveal,
We laugh occasionally at a joke, or mom's ordeal.

I may sound too harsh cause I never sustained a bruise,
By my courage seems dented, and I often seem to lose.

My moral fabric is sure, but my mind seems to wonder,
If I was somehow psychologically hurt, and my self esteem plundered.

I wish he would put down his book,
And open his heart, and take a look.

I've got resentment and pain, and feel left down,
Dad, we have time left yet to erase your awful frown,
Can we speak together, and rise above the ground?
Can we speak like equals?
Is there love left yet to be found?

My Lai, My God

And the bombs came,
And the bullets rang,
And the people cried,
The bullets sang,
The babies bleated,
The air was rain,
The Vietnamese screamed,
Gunned down in vain.

I watched it all, and said not a word,
I did not help, although I heard.

Night became like day,
Day became light night,
I tried to run away,
I tried to lose my sight,
I tried to ease my fright.

No panacea at all,
No Red Cross to right the fall,
Death the sentence,
One and all.

Olive Tree

When I let go of hate my brother followed in turn,
When I forgave my mother, my father came and learned.

When I give hugs to friends I create a special bond,
When I put out my hand to strangers I learned who I was.

When I do not envy my neighbor I notice what he needs,
When I see him the next day I ask him if he wants any seeds.

We planted a tree together, and shared the watching,
And it grew into a large olive tree, one that was truly something.

I watered it one day, and he gave it sod,
I turned the soil, and he came and trod.

Over time it grew, and gave us such sweet fruit,
And my neighbor became my friend,
And together we watched it bloom.

On Our Way

We're on our way,
To make the peace,
To right the wrong,
To set people free.

We've sent the troops,
We've packed their bags,
We gave them kisses,
And well wishes,
And saluted the flag.

We had a last meal of cereal, and lost moments,
Holding hands our thoughts like chains unbroken,
The time seemed so holy.

I checked my uniform for dust and wrinkles,
I checked my cap for starch and crinkles.

I hugged my wife, and kissed my child,
I said goodbye,
Hopefully for a very short while.

The plane departed,
The men were glum,
A patriotic song began,
But no one sung.

Outside the window the landscape disappeared,
And later the endless water was all I could see.

Then we touched down on the hundred-degree ground,
But my thoughts were in America, so far away right now.

The mission is peace in the Middle East,
The goal is something I know is very hard,
But I am a marine,
Proud of my country, my flag, and my God.

Our Streets Are Paved with Lies

Have you heard the news?
Have you heard them say,
You can find justice in America,
That is before today.

Streets are paved with gold,
That's what I was told.

Have you heard the news?
Have you heard them say,
You can find justice in America,
That is before today.

Streets are paved with gold,
That's what I was told,
You can make your dreams come true,
Well it's not always possible for me, or for you.

Color blind is also not always the case,
Racism is often on his face,
Death of an innocent he did embrace,
Nothing happened to the killers, a true disgrace.

Eye for an eye, or tooth for a tooth,
Will make the whole world blind,
And that is nothing but the truth.

Tell me Mayor D., will we ever know what happened?
Crown Heights is a reverse of the wicked R,
Our city, our country, is an old, warped, fluid-dripping, car.

Can we ever get together?
Can we ever love one another?

My faith in man is waning,
NYC living is so draining.

Should I leave this well-known place?
I would do it for love, law, peace, and grace.

NYC is often a very smelly pit,
Sometimes I want to have a fit.

I hate the violence,
I despise the hate.

Sometimes I want to run and hide,
Sometimes I cry, but like many New Yorkers,
It only happens inside

Peace in Israel

The lizard king sings no more,
The children and parents are taking to the street,
They are singing slogans in their quest for peace,
They are chanting, and bleeding pink.

I don't approve their methods,
I don't defend their cause,
But maybe, maybe, there should be some different laws.

I say the time has come for things to change,
I only wish other countries would help, and give up their rage.

I wish we all could go home,
I wish we all could live in peace,
I wish they didn't throw stones,
I wish we were truly free.

I used to think I was yeridah,
And Arabs were just a speck,
But I'm finding that we all need homes,
And that everyone deserves respect.

Meshtara and Shin Bet are doing what they must,
But I wish there was a better way to obtain others trust.

I guess it's hopeless, and "Democracy" prevails,
So be careful of the peace process,
Be careful of rocks, bombs, politicians, theories, and nails.

The Bitter Winds

I hear the winds calling,
Calling the voice of hate,
Ancient enemies rage,
Their timeless debate.

Shiite, Sunni, Palestine, Israeli,
North Korea, South Korea, Kashmir, Northern Ireland, Rwanda.

Their argument never seems to end,
No one ever seems to win, or becomes remotely friends.

They fight over land, identity, religion, and peaceful existence,
Words turn into daggers, thoughts into flames, and too often violent
resistance.

I read the reports of so many lives that were lost,
I saw all the bodies on the news, and futures that are naught.

I looked for someone to give me an answer,
As leaders often do the same,
And I looked into my heart,
As tearful mourners crowded the graves.

My hair is turning gray, and often falling out,
We need help here ASAP I wish I could shout.

The UN is really UNhelpful,
And I wonder where we're going.
I wonder and fear, and wish I knew what to say.

If we stay the course,
And our leaders do the same,
Will there ever be a winner?
For this siege, this quagmire, this never-ending game.

The Desert Wind

The desert wind is howling,
Or is it just behind my screens?
The desert wind is howling,
Or is it just in my dreams?

Hot air comes from the bank,
Cold air descends from up north,
But snow is not on the way,
Neither is the dove of peace,
She's not flying today.

No, the desert wind is howling,
Laughter is on hold,
The desert wind is howling,
But construction of the wall is coming or so I am told.

There is a storm coming,
Not tomorrow, but perhaps someday soon.

The desert wind is howling,
Or am I just hearing things,
The desert wind is howling,
There is a solution, because I can dream.

Truest Trust

It takes time to get to know a person, and form that special bond,
It takes time to get to know a person, and becoming close is sometimes hard.

For to really get inside the other involves a certain risk,
If I tell them how I feel I might be embarrassed, or end up feeling sick.

Oh what I did I can't believe I said it,
And each passing day you might even regret it.

However every day might also be one to grow and learn,
What kind of person you could become, and what others are worth.

So I suppose the way to proceed is to take little steps,
No matter how strong you feel today, let your emotions stretch.

Take calculated risks to see how far you can go,
Judge the pros and the cons for saying yes or for saying no.

And read their bodies, and listen to what they don't say,
Because bodies breathe less, but they can show you the way.

And don't overlook the things you wish you could,
Be realistic, but avoid saying " You" or "I should."

Take chances, and don't live life with too many regrets,
Just take your time, but please don't sit too long on the fence.

What's in Man Can Be Found in Middle America

What's in man can be found in Middle America,
Look around our country, and what do you see?
But every color of the rainbow looking back at me.

Hidden pastures behind the mills,
Conceal undiscovered bounty from the tills.

What's found in man is rich for sure,
After discovering it's love and warmth I know you'll want more.

Fields of wheat have been sown,
Man's true potential can't ever be known.

The variety of plants and animals reminds me of the diversity we find
in man,
Every ethnic origin and language, every size and shape,
I can't say I've always been fair,
I can't say I've always been generous,
But I hope I can cultivate these traits some day.

Ask the farmer who deals with the soil because he knows,
Huge distances between cities reflect the distance between men,
Robert Frost knew the truth,
We must work at loving our fellow man, and never preach hate.

Because new understanding and empathy can be reached,
If we remember God's creation, and nature's bounty,
Diversity is important to maintain the symbiosis of our world,
Tell someone he is special or unique.
Make a difference.
Why wait?

What's in man can be found in Middle America,
But most importantly if you truly look, it resides inside us all.

Chapter 3: The Environment

A Found Sunrise

If you listen very closely,
And slowly open your eyes,
You can experience it very clearly,
Every morning sun at it's rise.

Purple, orange, and a glint of green,
Are made daily by God's great machine.

You can taste it in the dew,
You can smell it in the air,
Sweeter than a sugar beet, and oh so much more rare.

It tempts the inner soul to go to heaven's gate,
To climb a forest tree, and share it with your mate.

Rainbows are infrequent,
Flowers come and go,
But give me a sunrise,
What a glorious show.

Breaths After a Rainfall

Breaths after a rainfall are wonderful indeed,
It warms the cockles of my heart,
It gives me what I need.

It clears the nostrils of my nose,
And makes my head feel light,
It clears my head of stress,
As my body becomes less tight.

Arms and legs moving so fast,
Oh what bliss how long will it last?

Where is the great cataract?
In heaven?
I want to walk through it,
And fall asleep in the cave underneath with God and his angels.

Do You Know Snow?

When there is snow on the landscape, spring is not far behind,
Though the sun isn't shining, it will appear in time.

To some snow can mean death,
To others a snow man, a snowball, a friend.

A blanket, a patchwork, a tent for the grass,
An annoyance, a bother, a pain in the ass.

Snow is many things,
The Inuit know it well,
So many names,
So many meanings.

Sometimes it laughs,
Sometimes it sings,
Sometimes it howls,
Sometimes it screams.

Have You Ever Seen a Snowflake?

Have you ever seen a snowflake on a cold winter night?
They kind of look like angels who will soon end their flight.

Each one is unique, and truly alone,
They are also like lost lovers silently returning home.

A snowflake by itself never causes any grief,
And if you ever taste one on your tongue, you'll find them quite sweet.

Add them to ice cream cones if you get the chance,
Put on Tchaikovsky, and watch how they dance.

Best of all is the glee that they bring,
Whether individual or together snowflakes are beautiful things.

Heaven's Appeal

The sky opened up one night,
And the heavens were revealed in all their beauty and delight.

The stars dotted the horizon like the specks of white in my eye,
They moved like a myriad of angels in a daily rapture.

Each one a different color,
Some were white, others green or blue.

Cassiopeia join together with Orion, and show him how to play,
Who are your friends tell me their names.

Old dipper and young are separated for all time, barely,
The bear doesn't care he just eats comets, and is fine,
All is quiet outside except for the chatter of crickets.

The atmosphere is blissful for I have not a single care,
What do you think of that?
Big sky, you are everywhere.

I Saw It All

I was there so that is why I know that
No ill designs were present, merely nature lashing out at the weak.

I heard the gale blowing, and it almost blew me overboard too.
The sound of the waves was deafening as they pounded the deck of
our dinghy.

You became more and more alarmed,
And screamed like animals when my brethren boarded your ship,
Searched you out,
Engulfed you,
You were frantic in your efforts, but we always win in the end.

We cover almost all of the earth so how could you possibly
Overcome us?
I watched your piteous plight, but I did nothing,
I would of have helped if I could, except I am only a raindrop myself.

King of the World

I see you,
I know what I did was wrong, and I'm sorry I made your life a
struggle.

What can I do now?
I can help you to the top, but it's not always up to me
Whether you'll stay.

I had to protect my territory you see,
I thought about the most important person, me.

And then you complicated my life,
In a moment of passion, survival instinct overcame me, and I lashed
out at you.

I realize now that I was wrong,
Because you were young, small, and vulnerable.

The world is cruel, and usually dog-eats-dog,
But here in our world, it's fish-eats-fish.

Nuclear Sunrise

The orange sun spread upon the horizon,
Hinting of warmth to come.
Like a peacock unfurling it's feathers,
Or snake shedding it's skin in the sun.

What will come of the morrow?
Will the world be here?
Or will there just be sorrow?
While the Russian scientists cheer.

Ode to a Weed

I see you weed not so far away,
I can tell already how long you will stay,
Your time is numbered anyway.

I respect what you give to our planet,
Even though generations of gardeners may not,
Oxygen, feed for cattle, and a whole lot more,
Can anyone say dandelions?

If only people realized that everything is important to someone,
That homeless man may have been a piece of grass in another life,
He just grew a bit out of control without anyone to tend him,
He just grew out of control without anyone to befriend him.

The planet is no different,
It is a gift to our children,
Better to give than receive they say,
Be careful with the spending it may not be here someday.

One Morning

One morning I awoke to find that the tree outside my window had
turned into a rainbow,
It pleased me greatly and above the rainbow I saw a second one with
children sliding down it's sides.

The tree then turned into a wishbone, and the leaves fell, fleeing like
desperate cicadas striving to return to the safety and comfort of their
homes, the braches.

I heard the wind blow that day,
Like the breath of an old man in a nursing home,
Or a patient in a hospital dying slowly of lung cancer.

It was dark so suddenly that I thought it was winter,
But it wasn't.

Only rain on a fall day,
Full of promise, but lacking compassion.

Orange Sky

The sky was orange,
The night was still,
The wind was silent,
There was a chill.

I walked the road to find myself,
I do it also to improve my health.

Who can forget he who made this place?
Who really knows if he has a face?

It would be nice to be our maker,
To bring forth life, but not the taker.

It would be hard,
That's for certain.

It's up to God to steer this ship,
It's up to us to take the trip.

Sailing away in the setting sun,
It's definitely hard, but it might be fun.

Our World

Our world is losing it's voice when automatic machines speak to our
answering machine, or to our voice mail.
Where are we going?

It seems fantastic, but people are losing their touch,
Technology is supposed to help/teach us so much.
Where are we going?

When people on a date or at the dinner table would rather look at their
cell phones, or Watch TV than talk. What does that say?
Where are we going?

If only I knew my neighbor, and he knew my child,
Could I pick up the phone, and give him a dial?
Where are we going?

If I knew his name could I give him a ring?
Could I say happy holidays, and would he say the same thing?
Where are we going?

If I was with my wife would I say, "I'll help"
If people really love one another why do they use their belts?
Where are we going?

If our world is so "nice" how come people kill?
Does our world have a future, perhaps with your help, it may still.
Where are we going?

If my baby is so beautiful why does she cry?
If babies are so beautiful why do people hit them, and sometimes die?
Where are we going?

If our world is so perfect can you remember when it was green?
If our world is so perfect are there wonders left to be seen?
Where are we going?

If our world is so bright why is the ozone so thin?
If our world holds so much promise, why do people starve themselves,
while others are so very thin?
Where are we going?

If our choices are different maybe we all can still win.

Power

I wonder if you ever think about the power we humans wield,
Power to destroy the earth,
Power to undue the miracles of creation and birth.

In six days the bible tells us the earth was formed,
Now, in six minutes it can all be destroyed
By a mad dictator, or two unhappy countries.

We all suffer the consequences,
So next time you see a bug flying in the air, or crawling on the ground,
Remember they too may have a family just like
yours waiting for them.

So think before you squash them,
Because we are not Gods,
Not you, nor I.

Queens Zoo Circa 1995

Where are they now?
Where have they all gone?
My friends have been replaced with weeds.

The winds blow along the slowly cracking paths un-walked on for so
many years,
So many years.

Only the roosters remain living on air,
Luftmenschen,
And the insects no food for so long,
For so long.

The joy that was so much a part of this place, and all the happy
children are long gone,
Long gone.

Only emptiness remains,
Emptiness and locked gates.

Money, or the lack thereof was the cause of this zoo's demise,
And instead of keeping the animals in their cages, the human animals
are now in their place.

Never to have freedom,
Never to know peace,
Forever crammed into smaller and smaller apartments until finally,
finally.
Where are we now?

Rain

Rain brings death to an unhappy few,
Rain is a savior, we know this is true,
To crops and cattle, and humans too,
It even forms the ocean blue.

Winter brings us ice,
Summer brings us thaw,
I think it would be nice,
I think it should be law.

Steppingstone Park

Mandnan's Neck,
That's what the Native Americans used to call it,
But I call it paradise instead.

I know it doesn't seem like Eden, but to me it means peace,
I come to the park to soak in some sun and feel free.

I come here to throw away my troubles,
To listen to the birds sing, and the roar of tugboats.

The wind chills me when the sun is gone, but truly feels refreshing
when it comes back,
Far away I hear children playing, and the sound of water lapping
against the shore, the dock, and the stepping stones.

The egrets wail for breakfast, lunch, supper, or maybe just a snack,
People walk on the dock to see the sunset, and sometimes stroll along
the beach.

No swimming though for years, it's too toxic,
Birds and planes fly together in the sky, but never compete here.

In the distance I see the lighthouse, the Bronx, and the mansions of the
rich.

The three wise men gather mussels, and hide under their ships for now,
The seagulls drop theirs from the sky to shatter, and then dinner is
served.

Families come together here by the Long Island Sound,
I hear a mingling of Farsi, Hebrew, Chinese, English, Spanish and a
few oy veys thrown in for good measure.

Otis Redding is in my mind, and so is bliss,
All the ships are gone today except for a lone power boat moored for
who?
And I try to steady myself against the coming storm.
I try to decide what I need to do,

47

Or maybe I just need some quiet.

Shut up helicopter!
The berry trees can't hide me, but bliss will return I'm sure,
Here at Stepping Stone Park.

I don't need one of their wonderful concerts today,
Just the sounds of nature around me, filling me, and I am content.

The Day the Shellfish Died

There they were washed ashore lying together arm in arm in arm,
Couldn't move,
Couldn't talk,
Couldn't swim,
Couldn't walk.

The sun was beating down, and the water was chilled,
The tides were out, and they might be killed.

Then they came and grabbed our ends,
They laughed and laughed, but they were definitely not our friends.

They kicked us, mocked us, pulled off a few arms, and threw us to the ground,
Don't you know we existed before you were walking around?

We've been hunted, and been eaten,
And lately taken quite a beating.

But we'll outlive you yet,
You're really not such a threat.

Just do us one small favor,
Humans, respect your elders.

The Rape of Terra

I've been raped.
I've been raped so many times that I've lost track.

I've been raped by people from all walks of life,
The rich, the poor, people of all colors, creeds, and religions.

I've been raped on the land, in the sea and sky without regard,
I used to be a virgin, but no longer.

There was a time when they honored me like the Native Americans
used to,
When they only took the fruit of my loins for a purpose,
But that day is gone.

My tears burn like acid, literally.
My heart is heavy, and decaying,
And I'm getting so very hot, I don't know how much longer I can take
it,
My name is Terra, otherwise known as your mother,
The earth.

The Sea

White caps top Long Island Sound,
As our boat is pitched round and round.

The air is calm, and the taste of salt is in the air,
How I long to stare.

To stare at the sea,
To stare at the shore,
I am never sated,
I always want more.

The ship is sturdy,
The crew is calm,
I feel so exhilarated,
I feel so free.

Inner peace suffuses the air,
Not a single care.

Overhead a bird flies looking for lunch,
It circles, it flies, and becomes part of the sky and sea,
The captain remarks, "A quasi philosophical religious experience is
now part of me."
I look up, smile, and simply agree.

There it Goes

The sun is warm in my room,
And I wonder what we will have to do soon.

It's getting much thinner out there,
High in the sky, the stratosphere.

I'm worried about what will happen you see,
I'm worried that someday we won't have it so easy.

They used to say the Bronx is burning, but now it's California, Utah,
and Arizona too,
Call it fake news if you want, but we all know it's the truth.

The nights are getting so much warmer,
The winters are fleeting,
And our snowcaps are receding.

The ozone is thinner than ever before,
The CFC's and coal plants are destroying it for sure,
The fridges and air conditioners are doing their thing,
And I hoped we would have learned to lessen their sting.

But progress is slow, and opinion as well,
I hope my words can ring the bell.

One if by land, and two if by sea,
What I see is going quick,
Do you see what I see?

Thoughts Outside

Walking, running, flying, spinning,
Oh, the world is beginning,
Billions of years who is winning?
God, What happened?
If this is a game what is the inning?

Are we on top or will we lose?
Will we blow ourselves up, or blow our fuse?

We've created the bomb,
We've created malice,
The two put together could blow up your palace.

Could reach the heavens, or warm up purgatory
Until the angels wings are singed,
Until Satan himself was burned to a crisp.

The end, a beginning, a cycle, a phase,
A trip, a path, a wild night destroyed in a blaze.

I whisper to the wind,
I call to the sky,
Lend ears to my sorrow,
Lend eyes to cry.

Traci Rimmerman

While lovers kissed the boat got closer,
While the wind blew it came nearer.

It crossed my line of sight,
The sails streamed by, but had no flight.

It moved on the power of gasoline,
Not currents, not wind, not even the human machine.

I smelled the scent of the sea,
But the gasoline was silent to me.

The ship dwarfed the others as it blew it's mighty horn,
Not of vengeance, not of frustration, not of scorn.

The birds circled, but drew no further,
The water moved slowly, and the white was mirrored.

In the distance I saw the city down south,
And on the water was reflected the land and myself.

I heard the crows, the crashing of waves, and the wails of children,
I heard my heart softly beating,
And the bliss of the moment was captivating.

Slowly, slowly, the ship faded away,
But the moment was inside me now, and would most definitely stay.

We Were Not the First

There was a time when there were no cars, and horsepower was
limited to one,
When Native Americans crisscrossed the land in more ways than our
complicated subways, or California freeways.

But the wild buffalo are almost all gone now replaced with nothing,
and I feel a deep sense of loss.

Time moves on, but in our attempt to escape foreign oppression be it
England, Russia, or whatever we enslaved the Indians morally and
physically, and put ourselves in a moral prison that we may never ever
fully escape.

Indian giver means more to me now than maybe what was promised in
the past.

Many tears have been shed, and not just on the trail of tears,
No, those tears were just the beginning.

If those tears were counted they might fill a lake akin the Dead Sea,
Interesting, Dead Sea, Indian Sea, I wonder what it could be?

I only know that the Indians, the original inhabitants of our country
will never roam the plains unencumbered, because unfortunately they
will never again be truly free.

God?

Hey God, are you there?
It's me do you have some time to spare?
I want to know if you really care,
To find out if you are more than just plain air.

From up high, higher than a bird can fly,
I want you to look at the world you created with your special eye.

It took you just six days to create it so I won't fault you for that,
But since then your people have grown lazy and fat.

Good and evil are represented for sure,
There are your angels, and those rotten to the core.

There are even those in between,
And I think *you* know who I mean.

But the plight of the planet is vested in us,
And I'm glad you've given us your great trust.

Can you ever forgive us for the mess that we made?
To cut down all the beautiful trees that once gave us shade.

We've polluted the waters and made the fish die,
You know God, I wouldn't be surprised if you broke down and cried.

All I want God is one more chance,
I think we're a good gamble,
I think we'll advance.

With technology I hope goes caution too,
I want the seas to remain being blue,
Have faith in us God and we'll be true.

56

Chapter 4: Hope

A Dream

Do you have a goal?
Do you have a dream?
A brass ring?
A fleeting scene.

A green light across the water,
But have no ship to sail,
A stone to be pushed for all eternity,
A task you will not fail.

A fantastic fire that burns bright inside,
Something you show no one, but do not wish to hide.

A dream written down, but locked in closets of doubt,
Something you wished people saw,
Something you wished you could shout.
Well, what are you waiting for?

It won't happen overnight,
Get started today,
Persevere, and you'll get over your fright,
That's all I have to say.

A Friend

Having someone to talk to
Is like two waves hitting each other,
They change in shape in form,
And will never again be the same.

Feelings expressed and new things tried,
Are always better than to be bottled up inside.

We can repent as Job one did,
But little can change if our feelings are hid.

How much better it is to have a friend to talk to,
Than to be ourselves and just yell,
In that case it might be easier to just use a well.

A Goal

A goal starts in the mind, but is kept in the heart.

It breathes it's own breath, and feels pain when others try to crush it,
But diligently and with the courage of the survivors of tragedies it
lives on.

Through the long haul like a marathon runner,
It plods and fights to the end.

Through dedication it lives and grows and finally blooms like a
dandelion without boundaries.

We too can attain our dreams by putting effort into every action, and
being proactive.

Believing in our own strengths, and not letting anyone or anything stop
us from getting there.

Dreams are ephemeral and leave after a nights sleep, but goals live on
and are ours to be reached, and can be.

A Morning Sun

A morning sun brings much to bear,
It brings bright light, and lightens our cares.

We forget our problems, and gain a new lease on life,
Our sickness fades, as does our strife.

Optimism has a new name called morn,
It's true what they say you can be reborn.

But only if you believe in the child,
And do as Montaigne said,
Each morn can bring you a smile,
As you get up, and rise from your bed.

Afraid of Failure

There's a fear that's going through my veins,
It's a fear of accomplishing nothing,
And the fear of what others might say.

I feel afraid of dying, and never accomplishing my dreams,
I compare myself with my father, all too often it seems.

And when I ask myself how to start my goal,
I grow befuddled and discouraged, and fear I'm growing old.

I look at others through rose-colored glasses,
I ask myself why can't I be with a partner holding hands or laughing.

I'm scared of being common,
I'm scared of dying alone,
I'm afraid of what others will think, say, and being walked on,
I'm afraid of many things I suppose.

But no matter all these scary thoughts I am unique,
And can reach some goals,
Who cares what others think,
I can be content as I grow old.

As long as I take steps toward a path that I think is right,
The opinions of others are weak and trivial,
And my mind gives me might.

And time will tell what is important and what matters most,
Time will tell how I can grow before I become a ghost.

Afraid

Being afraid isn't noble,
Being afraid isn't pure,
Being afraid is immobilizing,
Being afraid is hard to endure.

But harder than being afraid is doing the things we fear,
It lies in wait for you like a snake, but does his poison ever have a
cure?

The cure for fear is breaking tasks into steps,
And when they are broken so small it's no longer a mess.

Take the steps one at a time,
And the fear will vanish I promise, both yours, and mine.

Against All Odds

Against all odds I am high,
Against all odds I try to fly,
Like the eagles in the sky.

And this is something I need to do,
A thing that gives me pleasure, and that's the truth.

A chance, a risk taken,
A step forward, greatness in the making.

A beginning for me to try on a new skin,
A time for me to finally sing.

A glass of wine to quench my thirst,
A girl to kiss, or possibly something worse.

A soul to raise,
A song to praise.

A lake to swim,
A time to be in.

Against all odds I aim high,
And if I make it I will say,
A plus for me is my grade for flying,
And that is something no one can take away.

Breakfast on the Lawn

The sun was bright and it's rays were warm,
No one was around to disturb my thoughts.

The squirrels were nonplussed,
Just dining on acorns and grass,
And I looked and smiled, and waved as I passed.

Simple things are so special,
Time is fleeing like a flower's petal.

The grass is green, and the trees are blossoming,
Cherry blossoms bursting like roman candles.

The bitter winds have died,
Sad memories are fading,
As I go forward in my quest for happiness in this world.

That's what it comes down to it seems so computed,
Why is our world so convoluted?

Maximize happiness, and minimize pain,
So psychological, so what do we gain?

Love and hugs, and things that are worn,
Trying to be romantic, or even just happy in any possible form.

I find myself getting resistance,
From a world that admires strength and persistence.

I guess I am not in that classical mode,
I am a romantic, or so I've been told.

What is it then that I should go and do?
I hurt sometimes, and often feel blue.

Money, money, get a job now!
It seems so difficult, but in my heart I guess I know how.
I want to make something of myself,

Maybe even earn some reality show-like wealth.

I want the world to remember me,
I want to help others become the best they can be.

Memories fade fast, and life even sooner.
So what I will do is dream, and live and give the world what I can.

This world large and I am smaller, but as young children grow, I will be bolder,
I've matured. I've grown older.

Carpe Diem

I know I should be out today to feel the sun's warm light,
But my limbs are feeling heavy, and my body isn't right.

I know I should clean my room, and make things ship shape,
But this book is calling me, and saying to procrastinate.

My goals for the future, and those I plan for today,
Have grown in leaps and bounds, and I feel I am too late.

But, why can't I stop picking my nose and pick my brain instead?
To ascertain how I can get off my butt, and get on life's gravy train.

I read self-help books, and talk to those in the field,
I visualize what I dream of, and forgo expensive meals.

I take risks, but they scare me so,
I wish I could do one daily to help me grow.

Carpe Diem I think that's how it's spelled,
Is more than a word, it's a message I should tell myself.

I read success stories and books to improve, but I haven't found my
smile,
I know truly that wishing doesn't move us forward, but doing anything
is far better than living in denial,
I wish I could find true happiness, at least for a while.

Change of Scenery

Sometimes at night I am afraid of some ancient fear,
The dark carries with it strange possibilities,
Our choices can be terrifying,
Our way may be unclear.

As we walk the path to our own destination we cross many roads,
We see many sets of footprints,
But it is up to us to walk in them, or in white untouched snow.

Robert Frost might say that white snow untrod is clean,
Others could venture that it is easier to walk in well-worn paths,
Even the ones you've never seen.

The neighborhood track is easy to walk on, and is sometimes
Boring, but at least we know the depth of the snow.

But it is not hard to take a chance on a round track,
It's not really a gamble to walk on an oval path.

What is hard is to venture through that untouched snow, and go
walking off the track and on your own,
It's more exciting, possibly more inviting, but a long way from home.

Courage

What's courage to me, what's courage to you?
Each of us has a different view.

The sun inside that melts fear's ice,
The birds we hear that sound so nice.

A place to be, a place for me,
What is it that you sometimes see?

What is it that you really fear?
How come it's come so near?

Are there friends whom you could tell?
Are there choices that fit as well?

Can you fly away on robin wings?
Or make changes in anything?

Are you sure things are quite so bad?
Do you know anyone who's been this sad?

What have they ever done?
Is life ever *always* fun?

No, but we can make it together,
It can always be a little bit better.

On wings of hope we can fly,
Courage is the warm air that keeps us in the sky.

Different but Not

When I was born God told my mother I would be different, and I am.
The doctor handed me to her, and I'll never forget the warmth and
pleasure we felt at that moment.

These days that love has only gotten stronger,
But as I've grown older, I've had to fight to keep that spark from
affecting others.

I realize that I am responsible, and like a boy scout minding a fire
I have watched that flame inside me grow into a bonfire.

I've heard the jokes, the put downs, and we've cried,
But I have never let others who try to hurt me come inside.

And so I keep the flame lit for those I can trust,
And I've grown stronger till others remarks, and actions do not trouble
me too much.

And now I've arrived,
And thank God I'm still alive.

Others may have come and gone,
But my strength of will is still here, and my flame is still on.

Do You Know Who Your True Friends Are?

I'm you're friend,
I really am, and anytime you have a problem you turn to me.

Anytime you want to have a good time we're together, and
When you want to feel warm inside we kiss.

But now, you never seem to get enough of my love, and
You can't live without me.

You can't get me out of your arms, or eyes, or mouth, because
We're no longer two individuals,
Now, you are dependent on me, and I can't go anywhere without you.

I'm stuck, and
Only you can go.

If you found another who kissed as well you would probably turn to
them and leave me.

Don't get sick over me, because honestly I'm not worth it,
There, I said it.

Whew.

That wasn't that hard,
Was it?

There are many ways to find happiness on your own,
You could abstain and just say, "No." to me, and
Let's see how long our breakup would go.

You could find another way to boost your self-esteem like
Kissing babies, and making mother's dreams.

Try writing poetry, or watching the clouds go by,
Try watching sunsets, and observe the birds as they fly.

Pick a goal, and take a step,

Help others, and learn to be adept.

Be vigorous, and live for today.
Be close with your family and friends no matter what they say,
Admit that you have a problem with many things including me.

I'm really quite addicting so many folks can tell,
My name is alcohol please don't go to my well.

Don't Do It!

Don't do it!

Don't scream, don't hit, don't touch,
Your orchards are nearly in bloom don't uproot them because
They need your attention and love.

The problems that you have may not be what they seem,
Children are your escape, not the blame for your unfulfilled dream.

Pick up the phone and make that important call,
Get help for your problems, because they could be quite small.

Don't ignore them, and don't run away,
Face your demons, and make the most of your day,
Hold on, you *can* do it, that's all I have to say.

Don't Look Down Look Up!

Smile.

The important things in life are often not considered important, but they truly are.

Walk your own path to happiness.

But when you do remember to look up as you stroll because
You will notice people who love you, and the leaves on the trees as they come and go, and the changing seasons as you and they mature.

Smile.

And don't drive, walk, or do things too quickly, because time moves at the same pace always.

Learn the lessons of meditation and mindfulness.

Beautiful music doesn't change it's speed all the time,
Go slowly and appreciate precious moments, and always
Be open to new experiences and social events.

Because the people in your life won't always be there,
Love your family, and tell them you love them because they do care.

Say you are sorry if you are and remember
You can get there if you want to because you know the way.

Bad times often last the same as good,
But your mind makes it so,
Think of God too.

And when all else fails.
Look up and smile.

Don't Turn Off the Light

Don't turn off the light you have much yet to do,
The stars are always brightest on cold, clear nights, true?

You have people unmet never seen,
There are children unborn to be weaned.

There is happiness, love, and travel to and fro,
There are moments of laughter many more yet to go.

A light unlit will never cast a glow,
In darkness, it's brilliance will easily show.

Even for a moment, brief it seems,
Could change other's lives, and make other's dreams.

Be an inspiration instead for others anon,
Don't be afraid just leave the lights on.

Dreams

Dreams do not come true lying in bed,
Dreams do not come true when they remain in your head.

No, dreams are made by the force of will,
They aren't just given to us, no magic pill.

Dreams can be translated into our lives,
If we determine they are our soul's desire.

Fix them in your mind said Napoleon Hill,
And nothing can stop you, not voice, nor quill.

Drunken Stupor

When you came home last night,
Your appearance gave me quite a fright,
You were truly a sight.

Your eyes were red,
When you collapsed in bed.

Your breath was stinking,
We both know you were drinking,
And I've been thinking,
That our relationship in sinking.

So set yourself straight,
Don't even debate.

I need you too,
I don't want to lose you,
Signed, you know who.

Enough

I've heard enough,
You're too slow, too small, too qualified, too fat.

The man in the school said, "Get out!"
And I looked up at him, and I wanted to shout.

I wanted to say that you've just got regrets,
You've lost your dreams, and bowed to imaginary threats.

I wanted to tell him that life is a line,
I wanted to tell him of Picasso, Einstein, Whistler, and Milton who
was blind.

I wished I had said that things *can* change,
And that people with some work are able to overcome their rage.

Life is not making a mark,
Life is trying to ignite the spark.

Life is choosing a way to live,
Life is taking risks, and being willing to give.

I suppose that a full life is like a child of wonder,
Who picks up each thing, and slowly learns from his mother.

Delight of learning can be experienced by all,
Triumph is often evident, but not is the fall.

KFC was started by a man of sixty-five,
He didn't want to stop going, no, he wanted to be alive.

Face the Day

Face the day, face the day,
I don't know how to face the day.
I've lost my power, I've lost my way,
I've forgotten how to face the day.

I took a long shower,
I tried washing away my shame,
I don't know how to face the day.

Temptation is a struggle, and I thought I was stronger still,
But instead I'm hurt from falling down that hill.

It could be liquor or women that make us weak,
Help me please my options seem so bleak.
If anyone sees me and knows what to do,
Could you please give a hand I'm feeling oh so blue.

My family doesn't see it,
They think all is well,
They always see the good,
And I always feel like hell.

It's getting late it's almost 12 at night,
The day is coming soon, and I'm still not feeling right.

They say sleep helps our mood,
And so does extra light,
I will try my best again tomorrow,
Though I still feel the fright.

Face the day, face the day,
I don't know how,
I feel so ashamed,

But God is here, and he knows what to say,
With his presence my world seems less gray.

Faith

Faith is knowing someone is with you,
Whether it is God, a loved one, or yourself.

Faith is the belief that your dreams can often come true if you truly
want them to, and are willing to do the work to make it so.

Faith lives simultaneously in the mind, heart, and soul.

Faith speaks many tongues but they all say the same thing,
Forget the failures of the past, and enjoy each day's repast.

Know that you can triumph, and
Together we will achieve what you long for.

How do you want it in the mind or here and now?
Till the twilight's last glimpse fades gently from the ground.

From My Bed

Whether in bed or at home,
Whether in pain or in traction,
Whether your fault or someone else's,
Live.

Live because there is so much yet to do,
Live because there are family and friends that love you.

Live because your pain will pass,
Or you will rise above it, yes.

I know it's hard to imagine that it will end,
I know you wonder sometimes who are your true friends,
I know you are scared, and feeling spent.

But hold your hands above your head,
And pray to God for these difficult times to end.

He will hold your prayers in high regard,
He will comfort you from afar.

Open your mouth, your heart, your eyes, your mind.
Open your soul, and see what you will find.

Open your box of courage sticks,
And hold them close till they are fixed.

The one above who helps me now,
Help my family on the ground.

I will hold on with all my strength,
I will live on because of love, and your grace,
I will survive, because these are obstacles I can face.

Give Someone Hope

To give someone hope you don't need to know z through a,
You just need to know some kind words to say.

Like, are you feeling better today?
Bet you will when you hear what I'll say.

You can also write them poems you see,
Just make sure you learn a through z.

Then you should learn z through a,
Afterwards you can write an essay.

God

God, I've never been a religious person before,
But I need your strength to help me endure.

I am in pain, but it's not from disease,
It's because I can't meet my needs.

Obligations have grown incredibly fast,
And my courage is low, and may nearly have passed.

I am not happy that much is clear,
I am frustrated, and living in deep fear.

I want to survive, and I want to smile,
I want to move forward, and stop living in denial.

I know you can't give me a home in heaven,
I know I can't work there for even one second.

But if you could send me an angel with fire,
I could engulf my heart's desire.

I could stand tall, and face all my fears,
I could sing songs in my enemy's ears.

I could laugh and cry, and not really care,
Because God is in me and with me so what if life's unfair.

Thank you God I will make a mark for me alone,
I care not for anyone else's enchanted throne.

Grateful

Open your eyes my child do not close them when you cry, but
Listen to how beautiful your world is above your sobs.

Come here, yes you remember how to walk, and
Don't think, or better yet think, think hard.

Your parents and other family who love you,
Your significant other thinks you're pretty special too,
The people at work and school respect you.

Now you are covered.

New suns rise as the song birds sing, and you know there's always
laughter somewhere to be found.

Write all about it or about yourself,
And don't forget to take pictures.

Sex with your partner is there also,
And if all else fails your children can yet make you proud.

He Wished He Had Gone Directly Home

He wished he had gone directly home,
Instead of making a bad decision that he now has to own.

He gave the woman her money,
They did the dirty deed,
And now he lives with regrets that haunt his every dream.

He wakes up covered in sweat in the middle of the night,
And thinks of his awful choices, and feels a sense of fright.

I should have been more careful!
I should have used my head!
Instead he was reckless,
And now may wind up dead.

I wish I was stronger,
I wish I could go back,
But life doesn't work that way,
And unfortunately that is that.

And now that he's here, and desperately wants to live,
If only there were do-overs,
If only he could forgive.

What do you do when you make a bad choice?
Pick up the pieces, and ignore that inner voice.

Take a deep breath, and believe you can cope today,
Learn from your mistakes, and love yourself unconditionally.

Hope Is the Key

Hang in there, and the best will come to you,
Open your heart to those whose love is true,
Pretend you are in their arms again,
Expect to be there soon my friend.

I know you are feeling very stressed,
So are we all, I'm sure you've guessed.

Today we are all here,
Holding onto you my dear,
Enter and do not fear.

Know that we can make you strong,
Especially as time goes on,
Yes, you will feel better, and it won't take long.

I Can

I can't, I can,
I don't know what to do,
I can't decide how to reach, reach the simple truth.

But if I could I would reach,
For my dreams, I beseech.
I know, I can, but when will I get across the path?
When will I get across, and reach my repast?

I'm tired,
I'm spent,
And that's how I feel,
And I know I have talent, and I know that it's real.

I'm sad,
It's true,
But what can I do?
A little step seems so far, far from the truth,

I'm blue.
Not you?
Believe me it's true,
Help me, and tell me what to do.

Help me, your friend, because I can't get there alone,
But with your help we'll get there, and we'll get quickly home.
I know, I can, and that's the simple truth,
My dreams are close, and that's because of you.

My friend,
My hope,
My worries are at end,

And sad no longer,
I have reached my dreams,
Thanks to my friend.

I Must Go On

I opened my eyes to make a friend,
No birds came out it was the end.

No tulips opened no one cried out,
I certainly feel down and out.

But damn it now the sun is here,
And with such bliss how can I fear?

I must go on,
I must go on.

No looking back to what once was,
The present is mine so I must not tremble,
God is my witness I am able.

I must go on,
I must go on.

And so it worked out, and I didn't break,
I came out O.K., and I wasn't fake.

Happiness is possible after all,
Truth, bliss, and maybe love in the fall.

I Walked the Beach

I walked the beach to find a shell to keep,
But no matter how far I walked I could not find a representative of the
ocean deep.

One that sparkled or shone with fire, and that could be seen alone in
the dark sea,
I found out instead that nothing was more beautiful than what lay
inside of me.

A clam, a pearl of potential, lies in all of us you see,
They speak of one thing, what makes one truly you, and truly me.

When you feel hurt or sad try to harvest your pearly gift,
Because your treasure is enough to always bring a certain lift.

And if you can't find a pearl,
Why man give your imagination a whirl.

Think of all those sad faces that could use some cheer,
And if you found out how to change their lives you could cast away
your own fear.

A bit lip never bleeds forever, and a broken heart can be mended,
A broken pot can be put back together, and as you tap your inner
strength your troubles will seem like feathers.

Do not fear dying, or pains you imagine,
Just give of yourself, and anything can happen.

I'll See Tomorrow's Sun

I'll see tomorrow's sun that I assure,
It doesn't matter how much pain I must endure.

I feel like a painting because my limbs are attached to the wall,
But in my mind I am Monet, by a field of verdure.

Listening to Mozart instead of listening to others scream,
Picturing a different reality is something I dream.

I cannot hear my captors, but I hear them when they laugh,
And I think of my children, and I think of the past.

I think of God, the bible, and the book of psalms,
I think of heaven and Job, and the things I have done so far.

I dream of goals I will certainly attain,
I think of people I've met, and my last trip to Spain.

I remember family, and friends from the past,
I remember mistakes, and overcoming them at last.

I think of my wife, and the women I have known,
I think of lives I've touched, and the things I have owned,

But most of all I think of tomorrow's sun,
How warm it will feel, when I finally go home.

If I Were Not Here

If was not here I would miss my baby calling my name, and living on
my own,
I would miss getting married, and being the king of my home.

Times I traveled,
Times I gasped,
Times I cried,
Times I laughed.

Beautiful hills,
Beautiful views,
Beautiful women,
Whatever I choose.

If I were not here my family would grieve,
If I were not here there would be no chance to be me,
If I were not here there would be no chance to believe,
If I was not here I couldn't be free.

There is a point to living each day,
There is happiness in this world, and so much we can say.

There is hope yet if you persevere,
There is hope yet if you cope with your fear.

And the rewards will take you as far as you dream,
The rewards are internal, and plain to see,
The journey is worth it for you, and for me.

Is Money the Key to Happiness?

If money were the key to happiness
I could use it to wipe my tears,
I could use it to keep my baby warm,
I would make the world yell cheers.

Out of this hellhole called despair
Into the land of light,
Comes something to replace the hang noose and chair,
And make my future bright.

It's Hard to Be a Kid

It's hard to be a kid these days,
It's harder still when you are hurt for something that you say.

Hurt for what you do, and hurt for what you did,
Hurt for no reason, and hurt because you hid.

They hit, they yell, they cast you glance,
They hold you *so* close, but could you ever enjoy that awful dance?

Like a python and it's prey, what can someone trapped say?

Talk to a friend like a teacher, a coach, a priest, or some other,
They can really listen to your troubles like a devoted brother.

You think your life will get worse, but sometimes things get better,
Change your life, make that call, text, or email that letter.

Last Night

Last night I felt pain inside,
I thought my candle was out of fire.

I felt alone this weekend night,
I had no friends to calm my fright.

I had not one family member with whom I could share,
Only stories and movies to fill up the air.

And I questioned my existence, and debated my fate,
I didn't cry, but honestly I didn't feel great.

Thoughts went through me, ones I'd rather not say,
But today they disturb me more than a little way.

I feel good about who I am, and believe in what I can be,
But I wish that this could be a new beginning for me.

Here's what I came up with.

To light my inner candle,
Requires an inner peace of mind.

It means putting down books, and talking to locals,
It means standing up, and becoming vocal.

It means being focused on what I want,
It means accepting who I am, rather than who I'm not.

It means seeing failure as only a temporary setback,
It means courage to laugh at vices, self-acceptance, and getting back
on track.

It means learning how to recover my smile.
It isn't easy, but somehow, someway, I'll overcome my trials.

93

Memorial Day

I did not attend the Memorial Day parade,
But it wasn't because I had nothing to say.

It wasn't because I did not believe,
It wasn't because I did not value their deeds.

I had something instead that I needed to do,
I have some memories of my own if you want to know the truth.

I have made mistakes and blunders, and have ill spoken words,
I have hurt others, and made many things worse.

On Memorial Day when many mourn and feel blue,
Remember the person who is gone, their deeds, and what they mean to
you.

Never let memories of them grow stagnant or old,
Because the world can still be beautiful, and their story must be told.

A dream realized is a dream no more,
And memories can be pleasant or be quite sore.

What we do with thoughts will determine our way,
Our memories guide us, but we have the final say.

I did not attend the Memorial Day parade,
But now that it's over I wish that I came.

I wish that my thoughts could be filled with good cheer,
I wish that my life could be lived without fear.

The band played on,
The Merchant Marines proudly marched,
Time moved on,
And so have my thoughts.

Missing in Presence and Mind

I opened my eyes and glanced in my place,
But he was not there not even a trace,
I imagined I would see a glimpse of his face,
But tonight there is emptiness where before there was space.

I know he is gone for only a day,
I know he'll come back shortly to stay,
I know I should be smiling and gay,
But it's hard to be happy, especially today.

Moods are volatile, unpredictable, and strange,
As we lose our emotions to our fears, and our rage.

Anger into sorrow, sorrow into sad,
My God are we truly helpless? I wish we were glad.

Come home father we have more to do,
Come home father we all miss you,
Come home father we all love you.

Mistakes

I've made mistakes before I've made quite a few,
I've made many mistakes if you want to know the truth.

But although I've made them I don't cry or swear,
But each time I make one I stop, and wonder how, and wonder where.

I stop and think what did I gain?
You see nothing is all bad but thinking makes it so,
There is sometimes pleasure from certain pain, and even opportunities
to grow.

Mistakes are natural even for men and women of greatness,
Einstein, Edison, and Lincoln made making them famous.

Mistakes of passion, and mistakes of my career,
Mistakes have made me introspective, and helped me face my fears.

Taking risks and making mistakes go hand in hand,
But living for the day and taking chances has made me the man that I
am.

Not Hindered

He rolled his wheelchair on the floor like a locomotive going down hill
while his child watched it all with a Cheshire-like grin,
The basketball flew back and forth through the air with ease,
The moment was special, and time seemed eternal.

Vietnam was long ago,
A distant memory, but sometimes it reared its ugly head especially
during his dreams.

His son was here though, and that made him strong,
Tears were a thing of the past he hoped, and he felt nothing could go
wrong.

It wasn't that loud inside only harmless whistles, and the sounds of
screeching feet,
No rockets, no mortars, no yells of retreat,
No garbage thrown by angry people, or the feeling of defeat.

Mylai, Saigon, and pass the hash pipe were unknown here,
Just pass the ball, work it, and make the shot without fear.
No one cares if you have legs or not.

Love, warmth, my son, my son, I care for you so,
I cherish you, adore you, and savor the moments as you grow.

Nothing different do I want for you, except to be careful, and to
always be true,
Your mother is gone forever, but I am always here for you.

So don't you fret or have regrets,
Watch me spin! I'm really quite deft.

Not just on the court,
I've made it this far, and I'll make it farther still,
With you by my side we'll succeed at the game,
With you by my side, my life feels fulfilled.

Of Darkness and Saber Tooth Tigers

Late at night, when the wind is blowing gently, I hear the voices of my ancestors calling to me warning of darkness and saber tooth tigers.

I know those tigers are long gone,
I know their tusks are no more,
But there are other dangers just as real.

There are animals that walk on two legs with knives for tusks, guns for claws, and there are places that should not be trod and things best left unsaid.

Darkness can exist in the air or in the body, and it's often difficult to see in either one, but there is a light that will illuminate your way, Tame the ancient beasts, and put them to sleep.

Hope.

When the darkness is so thick and so strong that it feels like elephant grass, hope is the machete.

When you don't know what you will do,
When you are unsure how you will ever go on,
Hope can be your beacon, your lighthouse, your star.

Follow the light of hope until you reach your goal, your destination, your happiness, and rise up like Icarus's father, and be warmed by the understanding sun that erases all doubts and darkness.

Oh the Stress We Endure

The mind can often feel distressed from many things I'm told,
You can hurt for a very long time, and it can make you quickly old.

Stress can change you, and make you do awful things,
It confuses us, and can make even the loudest songbird reluctant to
sing.

But when you find somewhere to be by yourself,
Or in another's arms you can defend against negative thoughts.

That crawl over your brain, and make you insane,
To do this step back, and think about your pain.

Write down your problems, and prepare to be freed,
The solutions you generate may be just what you need.

Time heals all wounds they say, but a change in how we think may
help you cope with even the bleakest looking day.

One Small Step

Listen very closely, and your world will come alive,
You can hear your life's history as you walk in every stride.
Crunch, crunch, feet on the floor,
Crunch, crunch, feet on the floor.

The view from the hill is very clear,
The images are coming oh so near.
My life is passing with every step,
I'm seeing everything with a new found depth.

From flagless poles to darkened diamonds,
Things seem downhill, things are flying,
I'm picking up steam, and far from dying.
Crunch, crunch, feet on the floor,
Crunch, crunch, feet on the floor.

I'm approaching my goals, and getting closer with every step,
I'm not afraid of growing older, although vampires know it best.

I look forward to what I will get, and what I will become.
Crunch, crunch, feet on the floor,
Crunch, crunch, feet on the floor.

I've had my ups,
I've had my downs,
I've had my smiles,
And my frowns.

But in all the steps I've taken not one has been so great,
As the one I take tomorrow that leads to an unknown fate.
One small chance,
To help my life advance.

I welcome it to my very core,
A new beginning,
I feel reborn.

One Woman's Wants

Dreams are lost here in the light and the darkness,
A ram's head against the wall produces no effect,
But our children, they are our dreams, our hopes, our salvation.

Toil and hardship and waiting in the heat and cold,
Wind whips us, and of course we don't have any shelter,
But the life we lead is in many ways better than the past.

No poverty to speak of, less degradation, and best of all no dictator,
Things are better I guess, but I have little to say what.

I have friends of course, because misery loves company,
Every day I see them for a while,
Exchange pleasantries, but sadly there is no hope in their eyes either.

I know I can't expect the rage to be apparent, but death smells worse
on me, and overcomes the smell of sex.

Sex does replace the pain for a while,
My children though are my dreams, my salvation, my future.

Dreams do come true in America for some,
But for us dreams are lost in the light and darkness.

Pain

It comes, it goes, it's never the same,
I feel it in my heart, my body, and my brain.

I feel it in the morning, in the noon, and night,
I feel the pain so much it blinds my sight.

My stomach trembles, my body aches,
I'm not sure how much more I can take.

And when I see the doctor and ask what to do,
He says not to worry, and to stop being blue.

But it's hard to do the best we can,
To stand up, and take it like a man.

When you are out of breath, and feeling rather low,
It's difficult to see how far you can go.

But I'll tell you this if you listen very close,
Something I know, of which I don't want to boast.

I know the secret to live with pain,
And that is to help others deal with their strain.

And I find when I do this I feel better inside,
And I'm sure you will too, if only you tried.

Regrets

I've treated women badly,
I've tried to make amends,
I failed in both attempts,
I've lost both my friends.

And now that I'm a little older,
And shed a couple tears,
I've grown and cried in many half drunken beers.

A simple poet that is me,
Who hopes his soul can be free.

Pain released, and joy regained,
How can I ever be the same?

An open heart and a closed mouth too,
My fellow humans I hear you.

Always try to sympathize,
It's not that difficult I hope you realize.

Friends and family can help ease your pain,
They can make life a little less insane.

Soma and Psyche

The body is the messenger of the mind,
The mind is the captain of the ship,
Working together like oarsmen, but too often under the harsh whip.

A baby comes into the world without expectations,
We leave it too soon, and often with reservations.

An egg is perfectly oval from afar,
But close up it has ridges, and prominent scars.

We too must strive to develop outside and in,
We must look to the future, and not where we've been.

A strong body and a cultivated brain can help you do deal with a lot of pain.

When you are prepared to handle stress,
You will be able to deal with a difficult mess.

When faced with misfortune turn to soma and psyche,
Read a good book, or ride your favorite bike.

Listen to music and dance if you can,
Play with your children, or work on your tan.

Whatever can make you feel happy and strong,
Will give you the ability to hold out for long.

You will gain courage and a measure of success,
Your limits will rise even from great depths.

Your friends can be companions or not,
But they are there for you, and can do a lot.

Families care too and want to help,
They may not know what you want for yourself.

So take time to think how you can improve,

Go outside, and put on your exercise shoes.

Get out your library card,
Turn off the TV, and prepare to work hard.

Happiness is something that requires some thought,
It may be a slow process to reach, but it has to be earned it cannot be
bought.

Sometimes I Am Afraid

Sometimes I am afraid to go to sleep at night,
Sometimes I wake up in the middle filled with horrible fright.

I wonder about the things I've done, things I've said, and things to be,
I want to forget some days, and say instead, "That wasn't me!"

And then there are the times when we wonder where the day went,
And if I know what I want, why can't I be more confident?

Sometimes I am afraid, but who cares we don't know what we can do
until we try,
Yes, I'm afraid of failing, but there is no success without setbacks
from time to time.

The bigger the challenge sometimes the bigger the fear,
Happiness comes when we are unsure or afraid, but still persevere.

Sometimes I am afraid at night, but in the morning I try once more,
He who tries triumphs they say, and that's something that can help us
endure.

Sometimes We Just Don't Know

Sometimes we just don't know the beauty we may miss,
When we tell ourselves not to take that scary, scary risk.

When we look at them later we smile, and shake our head,
And wonder why we ever stayed so long in our bed.

A new day brings challenges to those who seek them,
A new day brings hope to those who meet them.

You don't have to work as hard as ants to fill your day with beauty and romance.

A simple bird flying, or a day in the park,
Holding hands in the moonlight, or better yet in the dark.

But definitely seek passion in something that you do,
Don't worry about other's opinions of you.

Don't feel you have to be a renaissance man,
But if you desire it, know that you can.

Live life to the fullest try not to always say no,
Don't live with regrets, because they are poor seeds to sow.

Instead plant a crop that you want to sprout someday,
And if you plant them in enough places you'll be triumphant in *some* way.

The smile that comes with joy is as big as the largest success,
And who but you understands, and who but you can laugh.

The Complete Circle

There comes a time when young meets old,
When life's circle becomes complete,
Treasure your time the baby is told,
And never accept the word defeat.

Enjoy each day as the first,
Walk among the people as their friend,
Treat your children well, so they never have to know thirst,
Enjoy yourself to the end.

We are very similar you and I,
Both in strollers,
Depending on others,
It makes us want to cry.

So my last words to you as I close my eyes,
Never be afraid, and always be a person who tries.

The Definition of Fear

Fear is not just the unknown,
It's not just a walk in the dark, or the sight of a rat,
The claustrophobic feeling of a cave, or heights, or phobias,
Or that desperate feeling when a loved one is hurt or ill.

No, fear is much more,
It's a wall, a fortress, a medieval castle,
A wall longer than the one in China, and
Sometimes I see no end to the one inside me.

We can touch the Great Wall in China if allowed,
But in us it is but a dull ache, a fist in our body,
A pit in the stomach that cannot be assuaged.

A fighter feels the same pain, but only bleeds inside,
That, for me, is the definition of fear.

The Direction Ahead

The moon is bright tonight, but my goals are brighter still,
My heart is beating quickly, will me dreams be fulfilled?

I have no mentor, no compass, and no sign,
I have no one to tell me if I'm going astray, or truly doing fine.

My poems could be flat,
My rhymes could have no reason,
I could be out of whack,
I could be out of season.

I read many books, and I ask around,
I try each day to reach my kingly crown.

I compare myself to others, a crime I know is wrong,
But in my defense I only know how to sing one simple song.

And I hope with time I will learn a new course,
I promise to try another if only I have the force.

So, do not aspire to be someone else no matter how
Good their life seems,
Because you and I are different, and we all have different needs,
We all have different dreams.

Don't worry about what others may say, or even what they think,
Just be yourself, and don't be afraid of appearing meek,
Don't be afraid to attempt the goals you seek.

Because true power is present in us all,
Sleep tight, be courageous, and always stand tall.

I am myself, and I am no other man,
But I am more than just my name I am a man with a plan,
I believe in me, therefore I can.

The Great Abyss

We stare into the great abyss, and never know if it's emptiness or bliss.

Whether viewed from up or from down we all respect the holy ground.

Dust we were and dust we'll be,
God created man to be free.

Free to believe in our potential,
Free to know that we are special.

Before we sink into the abyss,
Remember to explore the subtle mist.

Mist on the mountain of dreams,
That surrounds our lives, and often looks like steam,
Try to peer through the mist of dreams,
And as you do your life may be redeemed.

The abyss is really not so dark,
It can be breached if you have the heart.

Oh subtle mist I challenge you,
Oh hope of mine you will come true.

Fearlessly we reach towards a dream of the past,
And now we are happy, and now we can laugh.

The Green-Eyed Monster

I feel a poem coming on,
It's about the things for which we long.

I see the lovers holding hands, and wish that it could be me,
I feel anger welling up so harsh and rapidly.

But it's hard to be objective when you experience a single slight,
It's hard to have perspective when you think it isn't right.

The couples may be casually walking, or kissing on the bench,
And I feel that it should be me, because I know I am a mensch.

So many beautiful women on the street, in the restaurant
Or in my class,
It hurts sometimes to know they are out of grasp.

My brother says try the Internet there are many women to choose,
My cousin scores all the time, and never seems to lose.

I have dated women and know what that means,
But too often love is stalled, like many unfulfilled dreams.

I can do more to make my life complete,
I have to try again, and believe I can succeed.

The Joy of Life

The paths we take in life are not always steady they are like walking
on a moving dock, sometimes difficult but possible.

Whatever decisions we make we must remember that life goes on, and
to stop sometimes and watch our children play,
Appreciate the lessons they teach us to not to take life so seriously.

Time moves on no matter what we do.

Rocks are still weathered by the sea,
And though our lives have meaning, we are not omnipotent, and
should not worry about having to be.

Children teach us something else,
To enjoy what you do, and find people that share your passion.

Do not worry about failing, because there is no real failing in life only
making efforts.

Success is subjective, and that love comes from inside first.

Smile at least once a day if you can, because time may only be here for
today.

Enjoy it.

And if you still are not happy, find your purpose ASAP.

The Lady in Black

Her name is despair,
She's the keeper of light,
It doesn't seem quite fair,
It doesn't seem quite right.

She takes away your happiness,
Her laugh is cold as night,
You might be tempted to kiss her face,
But like a canine she would bite.

Who will come and rescue me,
And restore my faith in love?
Who will be my curing grace?
One small white dove.

The Power of Family

Sometimes we forget the power that families bring,
When we are together that sum is greater than all the parts.

Sometimes we don't know what to say, and we aren't always tactful,
But our love is real, and our concern genuine.

And how we wish we knew how you felt,
We bring gifts that we hope you will need.

We bring cards with well wishes of our hopes and concerns,
But most of all we bring love, and if you could just open your eyes,
You would see so many people that care and that's no lie.

The phone could ring all day from the ones who love you,
And to bring a smile is gift that can bring quite a lift.

We do it because you are worth it,
And even if you don't believe me now, someday perhaps you will.

Realize that we are thinking of more kind words to say.

A family chain is made of many strong loops,
And you, my love, are an essential part, and that's the truth.

The Saddest Picture I Ever Saw

The saddest picture I ever saw was of my friend when he was three or four.

He was riding his father's shoulders, and exuded a sweet smile,
No one could possibly know it would end in a short while.

He died inside his car you see,
He didn't believe he should go on and breathe.

He didn't think life had any meaning left,
But when we saw his pictures we all felt bereft.

And yet I see him every once in a while,
He is on the face of people who rarely smile.

I don't always need to see their faces or hear them when they speak,
I just look at their bodies, which always talk to me.

And when I get down I think of the sadness his death brought,
I think of my life, and all that it has taught.

So instead of doing something rash I call family instead,
But inside I wonder who is really at their end?
Who could really use a friend?

That's why I keep on writing to save even one life,
The Talmud says it can save the world, and somehow that would make things right.

The Source of Life

The source of life lies not in bread, but in faith in God,
The weak and strong may soon be dead in earth that we trod.

But if they choose to take their chance on this planet now,
Surely they will meet his angels nearby on the ground.

To reach their goal, and try their luck,
I do not know what may grow,
So I say take the chance, you know, what the @#$%!

What Now?

The sunlight disappeared, the ice filled the trees,
I watched it from my window, I saw it and was pleased.
The train moved quicker then,
But now it snakes along,
The dark reveals no beauty,
The land is all but gone.

I've read all the papers,
And put aside the weekly,
I've tried to make conversation,
But everyone is sleepy.

I've tried to take a rest,
I've tried to close my eyes,
But my mind keeps jumping,
Though I try and try.
I've made jokes to women,
And laughed and listened to them complain,
I've waited in lines for hours,
To win some silly game.

And now I'm heading back,
Back to status quo,
My eyes are truly heavy,
And my dreams have long to go.

I see lights in the distance,
And further when in flight,
I try to heal the world,
I want it all tonight.
I want to reach my dreams,
I want to win this fight
My journey has begun,
My goals are within sight.

Willy, Can You Hear Me?

I wish I knew the pain that you felt,
I wish I could have heard your silent yell.

I wish I heard the signals that you gave on that last night,
I wish I could have recognized your dire, dire, plight.

Sometimes I wish I were stronger, more knowledgeable,
And more empathetic,
Sometimes I wish I had told you more often that you were special, and
definitely not pathetic.

I wish I had told you that no one is perfect,
I wish I had told you that you are wonderful for certain.

I wish I had told you that people love you,
And how many people cared and were devoted.

I wish I knew you better, and the difficulties that you faced,
I wish you talked to me or to a therapist, and we were able to set you
straight.

I wish I was a better writer, and could have made a difference,
I wish so much that others could really hear you, and not just pretend
to listen.

Sometimes I see you in places you cannot be,
I know you are sleeping in the kingdom by the sea.

In my heart I will never forget who you were,
What you did was your choice, but I wish you knew that life is worth
living for.

Chapter 5: Other Poems

A Day in the Life of Salem, Mass.
(To be sung to the tune of Copacabana)

Her name was Hester,
She wore a letter.

But that was 300 years ago in a place I didn't go.

His name was Dimsdale he was reverend,
And he wore a letter too, and he wasn't very true.

And there was Pearl she was a girl.

Beautiful beyond a mother's dreams, or so it seemed.

Music, adultery, and passion were never a fashion,
In Salem, Massachusetts.

A Reef

You've passed me a thousand times,
And never given me a second look.
That's part of the problem, because too many of you have ignored me.
You're always in such a rush, or probably just on your phones.
I feel your pain,
I really do.
Last month in your fit of rage I didn't strike back,
But your attack caused me to self-destruct.
I stood by passively, and in a moment you were gone.
I was hurt a little, but you were really the one who suffered the most.
If only you had known that there are many of us who care,
We don't just sit around, and watch the world go by.
We are here for you all the time.
I'm sorry for your family's pain.
I'm sorry you died beside me.
I'm sorry you didn't recognize me for who I am, because you were
drunk or distracted.
I'm sorry you couldn't live with yourself.
I'm sorry you drove into me.
No longer just a tree, but now a reminder

A Rose Can't Grow in Polluted Soil

A rose cannot hope to live in polluted soil that has no nutrients,
It needs nurturing and clean water to develop, not dirty.
Roses cannot scream when enough has been enough,
They can only shed their petals,
Point their thorns,
Their screams come and go, but things are still the same.
The rose remains the same size it was before.
A rose needs a garden and a special gardener to grow best.
I would gladly give my petals and exchange my soil for love, and
someone who cares.

A Shot

A shot rang out in Philadelphia,
The car didn't stop, but their hearts did.
No reason at all for the madness,
No reason or cause,
No drugs, no women, just death.
The wild streets of Philly.
And although we could not hear the shot, or feel the cold bullet pass,
We read the pain in their faces from the photograph in the paper on a
Sunday afternoon over bagels, and large glasses of orange juice.

Amazon Memories

I'm floating in the deep waters of the Amazon,
I gaze overhead at the parrots watching me, mocking me.
What are they saying?
Or am I back in my mother's womb all warm, cozy, and protected?
And no one can harm me except her of course.
Please mom no alcohol tonight,
It stings,
You don't need it, and I sure don't,
I'm not legal to drink yet.
I feel a sense of tranquility, and hear a quiet hum,
The movement of the water is gentle, calm, and relaxing.
All my thoughts are frozen, and only calm remains.
The warm water relaxes me,
Freezing the demons, freeing my tensions, freeing my mind.
Am I in heaven?
Have I gone full circle?
Does God have one large bathtub where he creates life?
Wouldn't that be cool?
I wonder what then?
Fill my tub to the brim.
Water is often life or death,
It has brought both to some,
The choice is often not yours,
God fills the tub, or drains it.
Your only choice is to swim or not.

Bubble Trouble

A blown bubble is a beautiful sight, but alas for too short a time,
A young child is wonderful and perfect, but alas for too short a time.

Like children bubbles have to be made,
Like children bubbles usually fade.

It's easy to make bubbles when you know how to do it,
It's just as easy to have sex, and then rue it.

Bubbles break if you blow them too hard,
Children hurt if you hit them too hard.

Our goals as parents is to give time to our tasks,
Blow on our bubbles gently, and watch how they dance.

Speak to our children with words of praise,
Hold back the anger, and instead give them a gaze.

Watch how they grow, and listen to what they say,
Like the bubbles they won't be always here to stay.

Make time for them and play when you can,
Because life is short before the boy is a man.

The girl is a woman already in full bloom,
And it seems like yesterday they were asleep in their room.

Jack and Jill are names for bubble soap,
But they are also children's names so don't be a dope.

Hold them close, and kiss them again,
Be warm and always be there as their friend.

Love is not a four-letter thing,
It means oneness, and that you're special to me

Bliss at Last

While you were sleeping in bed,
Images of crumb cakes dancing in your head.

I was out exploring the streets,
Eagerly awaiting whatever adventures I might meet.

The church bells rang,
The water ran underground,
The crickets sang,
One small sleepy town.

My step was light, and barely left a print,
My breath was crisp, because winter had left a hint.

I drank it all in like a sponge collecting a spill,
Tranquility at last, I can never get my fill.

Truly peace of mind my aching joints forgotten for now,
The holiday spirit is here, and how.

Sadly my journey has come to an end,
The stars were my guides,
Tonight they were friends.

Brother

Through the many years I've known you,
Whether near or far,
You have been so special to us,
Because of who you are.

You've taught us to appreciate simple things like a movie, a moment, a
joke, and I look up to you, more than you'll ever know.

So now that you're at a milestone, and thinking about your life,
I hope you realize that you are a great brother,
And husband to your wife.

A great father to your children,
And son I am sure,
And will always be number one,
In our family of four.

Covenant House

There are many openings on my face,
There are several windows of opportunity,
The choice is yours,
We are always open.

Come in if you like, and stay for a while,
Leave if you must, but you never have to hide.

Please don't hesitate to come through our doors,
Nothing violent, of this we're sure.

We welcome you all,
Come in peace,
In a thousand different languages the message is the same.

128

Falsely Accused

Walking down that long aisle,
Whistling songs all the while,
On the way to my trial,
Question is who to dial, and what plea to file.

The guards are yelling jeers,
The prisoners are giving me leers,
And in it all stands my solitary mother in tears,
Don't be afraid she says you'll always be my dear.

Cameras are flashing like a sea of stars,
Their blinding light like a caravan of cars,
At least I'll never again be behind bars.

Was that the sound of applause?
I wonder, what was the cause?
Please God no long pause.

The verdict is in,
I knew what it would be,
I knew they would *never* set me free.

Not to say that I feel guilt,
It's the scales of justice that are tilt.

It's not a trial it's a show,
To the chair I must go,
One last word, and that is no!

Feet

We never think much of our feet,
Except when we've slumbered, and find them asleep.

Feeling like we've got pins in our toes,
Or no feeling at all like when you wear too many clothes.

I really do treasure my gift of motion,
And the ability it gives me to swim in the ocean.

To walk on the sand, or to walk on the shore,
They're what God created them for.

Tickle one when you get the chance,
And watch with pleasure how that person will dance.

Two really are plenty for me,
They allow me to explore the world and be free,
What should I do next walk or swim in the sea?
What does it matter I can be me.

Freida: Gone, but Not Forgotten

What can we say about a relative that has died?
Except that we'll miss them, and that we cried,
The doctor looks sad, and says he tried.

When life ends the soul is reborn,
It kindles anew, and changes its form.

To heaven it goes like Icarus once did,
But this one stays and cannot be rid.

On earth we mourn for the soul that has passed,
But we know in our hearts that her die has been cast.

When we think of her and how she was kind,
A greater soul than Freida's would be hard to find.

Home

Home.
Home is where the heart is,
Home is where I live.

Home.
Home is a term for a feeling that we share,
Home is tranquility, and a breath of fresh air.

Home is downy quilts, and soup when we're sick,
Home is family, fireplaces, and several warm drinks.

Home.
Home is where our children learn and grow,
Home is a place that I long to go.

Home is memories, pain, and pleasure,
Home is like Sunday mornings after any kind of weather.

Home.
Home is a place that I will one day leave,
A home of my own that I will make for me.

A home is unclear and must be made from scratch,
Home is sometimes temporary, but for others it's one that will last.

Home is roots and more than just granite,
Home is where the soul resides, any place on our planet.

Home.
Home is a great four-letter word that should rhyme with love,
Home means a peace that we all should know.

Home is who we are, where we've been, and who we'll be.
Home is with us wherever we go, and with that feeling we'll always be
free.

The Hunt for Love

Have you spent your day,
And not admired the sky?
Have you thought to yourself,
I don't know why?

Stone and steel replace gardens and grass,
The hurried pace,
How long will it last?

What about this thing called love?
Have you found the person you've been thinking of?

Have you longed to have them,
But only found them in your dreams?
Can you feel their touch,
How real it all seems.

I've hunted for my love like a hunter hunting game,
I've found it more elusive,
It's driven me insane.

Just when I think I have her, my trap is full of holes,
Just when I think my arms will hold her, she's gone to where no one
knows.

Oh beautiful bird return to me and give up your protracted flight,
Come back to me and live with me,
I'll love you every night.

I Am Free

I awoke to a peaceful world,
Where children play, and all are friends,
An endless sea,
A forest green,
All joined in hand,
All sing with me.

I am free,
I am free,
Like the bird who leaves his tree.

Love abounds, and fills the earth,
Can't get our fill,
There is no dearth.

Thank you God,
Thank you all,
Together we shall end the hate.

We are free,
We are free,
No more hate,
We are free.

I Love You

It's hard to fit my love on a sheet that's 8 by 10,
Because I love you so much, and your more than just a friend.

I could categorize the things about you that fill me with pride,
I could make long laundry lists of my feelings inside.

I could fill a dictionary with words of how I feel,
But I would rather tell you that I love you, and that my feelings are real.

You are sunshine and perfume and a tasty strawberry pie,
You are a blessing, a comfort, and so very warm inside.

You are an ear, a smile, a midnight breeze,
You are my doctor, my accountant, my lover, and my dream.

You are soft like a dandelion, a sea of emotion,
My love is drawn to you like rain to the ocean.

Your blue eyes are beautiful like a newborn child's,
And when I see them I notice a reflection of my smile.

I hold your body close, and hug till we're content,
I will love your forever, and my love will never end.

I Remember Great Neck

I remember Great Neck,
Sleeping with the window open listening to squirrels, crickets, cicadas,
and an occasional car.

Sitting at Stepping Stone Park watching the sailboats, egrets, and
Canadian geese go by.

Feeling the gentle breeze and listening to the sound of waves with my
legs up on a chair while I read self-help books.

Walking down the dock to see the sunset, the lighthouse, mansions,
and Co-Op city in the distance.

Walking the lanes at Parkwood Pool, playing sports till dusk, or tennis
at Allenwood Park with my brother Bruce, and never feeling tired.

The library looms ahead by the bridge with pussy willows beside and
beneath her.

Sitting in the stacks reading Leon Uris and Steven King when I was in
High School when really I should have been working.

All my school time behind me, blurred, but sometimes with moments
of clarity of highs and lows.

Temple Israel for helping me learn Hebrew, get a Bar Mitzvah, and an
understanding of my religion.

Middle Neck Road, Wimbleton and Brokaw Lanes, my rooms, and
fond memories of Passovers past, and thanksgivings too.

Laughing, laughing, laughing, and a few cries too.
With my brothers, sister, parents, and nieces, and in-laws,
With memories like these, who could ever remain feeling blue.

136

In the room I Saw

In the room I saw the woman without a whit of waiting,
Down the curved road I saw the man contemplating.

I heard the laughter, and saw him smile,
What a contrast with his fast-talking guile.

The helpful sprite, the mean spirited man,
The rolling eyes that kicked the can.

And birds sung out like crows of yore,
And I meditated while my father snored.

And Dr. Seuss wrote a new verse,
And my friend Willy was too early for the hearse.

And the fish tank stank, and soon the fish died,
And Curt Cobain lived in true denial.

And I escaped it all in my writing,
And my throat was sore, but I didn't feel like crying
.
And Mike Waxman came home back from his extended dream,
And I wonder if I will see what I want to see,
And be what I want to be.

And still I try to make a path,
Blindness is created, and so is my wrath,
But I will write by candle light too,
I will write on till I am through.

Lady Singer

I've seen her before she's always the same,
All full of smiles to cover her pain.

She tells you her tale every weekend at night,
And you come back for more to gaze at her plight.

She's past her prime, but she'll never tell,
Cause she's young inside, and living so well.

Her hair looks the same as it was in her youth,
As she resonates her voice throughout our nine booths.

I glance at her face every once in a while,
I don't really know how she manages to smile.

I guess she's enjoying her self,
Not really worrying about gaining much wealth.

Artists are a strange lot for sure,
But I would trade my cars to be happy and poor.

Mom's Secret World

It's dark in here will someone please turn on the light,
It is really dark in here, or do I lack the power of sight?
It definitely leaves me with a sense of fright,
To be unsure of whether it's day or night.

It is warm though and peacefully still,
The tranquility of it all, I can never get my fill.
If I am thirsty or hungry sustenance is always there,
I have few worries when I am in my mother's care.

There is some noise it sounds like voices to me,
I'd like to respond, but I can't I'm not free.

I think I'll go swimming, "Yes," that's what I'll do,
Although it's strange this sea is black instead of being blue.

I can't swim many laps I seem to be anchored in somehow,
At least I can stretch my legs to tell her I'm in the prow.

Now? No! This can't be happening it's much too soon,
I never dreamed I would leave this beautiful lagoon.

With every passing second my world is getting bright,
I hear many voices are they aware of my plight?

I'm coming out of my deep ocean blue,
It almost like I'm surfing if what they say is true.
I'd like to see this world, but my eyes are shut like glue,
Ouch! They're jabbing me with needles to ward off the flu.

Get your hands off my ass I think you've had your fill,
Now that you're done could you please leave, because I'm feeling ill.

Ah, hold me momma, and squeeze my body tight,
And promise me you'll never let me out of your sight.
All I need now is one small kiss,
Mother, oh mother, your infant son is in bliss.

139

Moving Out

The chrysalis opened,
The butterfly flew,
I watched agape,
But I knew.

It was time,
Time to move,
It was time,
Time to shoe.

I packed my bag,
I loaded my things,
I drove my car,
I moved in.

It was so small,
Like Harry's cupboard at best,
But I smiled at what I had,
It was what I wanted at last.

I picked up the phone to call a friend,
The couch was soft and I was content.
The clock struck two, and I was done.
It was chosen, and I would certainly have fun.

The struggle was new, but one I believed,
It was all new, at least for me.

And when I think,
Where I was,
I was pleased,
That I am loved.

The party was grand, my friends are sure,
I am lucky,
To be amored,
I am lucky, because I've endured.

My Mom

I hear soft music wafting from her mouth as she recites the tunes that
make up her soul,
It does not matter that she cannot read the verses,
It does not matter that the words are not correct,
What matters is her firm desire to show her strength in her song.

If you were to hear her sing you would think angels had landed,
And were speaking directly to God.

I have not seen many doves in my life,
But every week at temple I hear one,
How could you not love a person as beautiful as my mother.

Sister

I have but one sister, and she stands alone,
My sister is wonderful, and this is universally known.

And as she approaches her birthday,
Let me rejoice, let me say,
You have been so terrific to me in so many ways.

Listened when I have felt down,
And for a quick pick-me-up with your kids, husband, and dogs around.

I appreciate all your advice,
I can see you are a wonderful mother, and wonderful wife.

And been a great sister, and taught me many things,
You are more precious to me than rubies, or diamond rings.

And I love you dearly, and wish you only the best,
You are getting better with time, of that I can attest.

Never a Smile

Ever notice a "bum"
Sometimes with rum,
He always looks glum.

Never a smile,
In a long while.

He sleeps on the street,
Shoeless his feet.

Nowhere to go,
Except skid row.

Yes, friends it's true,
It's not funny when they're blue.

So give a little money to him or a charity,
Maybe he'll be happy someday
.
With our help I hope so,
Let us help,
Let us pray.

Nightingale

Crickets chirping.
Willows cry.
Stars so bright in the sky.

The moonlight glistened,
The air was still,
I watched it all and drank my fill.

Next morning I awoke to find you by my side,
Warmth so intense you make my body come alive,
Open your eyes my gem, my prize.

Awake to my kiss,
Bring me my bliss,
You're sight do I miss.

You're breath is like the playing of violins,
It rises, it falls, again, and again.

Your hair is like yellow gold,
Your lips like rubies.

When I am with you I feel wealthier than the richest king,
Oh darling awake, oh nightingale, please sing.

Not Enough Change

Young man, young man, what is it that you have there?
Two six packs of soda, and no money to spare.

Those aren't the cheap ones, those aren't on sale,
The boy looked puzzled, and body seemed frail.

She smiled and pointed to go to aisle eight,
He quickly flew there without a debate.

Are you from the projects? She asked with a smile,
Yes, he said without a hint of denial.

She empathized with him she had been there before,
She lived there once, and had always wanted more.

You don't have enough change I can't make this sale,
His young face blanched, and body turned pale.

She changed her mind, and gave him a wink,
Just don't tell my super you know what he would think,
He would come over and make a big stink.

The boy was grateful what more could he say,
Except for a simple thank you it brightened his day.

One small act can mean so very much,
I was touched by the moment it was something I could clutch.

Then he was gone and out of my gaze,
I wonder if I could get her a raise.

Perspective of the Ant

There you are towering above me
Rarely aware of my plight below,
Unaware of my toils and hardships or my daily grind,
Concerned solely with your problems and flights of fancy,
Well, look at me!

I carry more than my share, and do you ever hear me complain?
Even if you can't understand,
I work well with others do you?

Work for the greater good as if our lives depend on it,
And often they do.

What are the results of our great civilization?
Yes, some of them have been destroyed, but then again so have some
of yours.

What you must remember my friend is the lesson of the ant,
A lesson of the determination, and that miracles *can* happen when you
least expect them.

Always remember that, and never underestimate the power of a good
day's work.

Never, never, think you can squash the working man like a bug,
because we will always endure.

Promises Kept

Hitler, Stalin, Genghis Khan,
Aristotle, Galileo, they are all gone.

The evil, the good, the wise, the dumb,
They've changed our lives, and how we look at sun.

It's risen, it's fallen, they're gone, they're over,
White dwarf, quasar, pulsar, supernova,
Planets, stars, Roman gods, the evil that men do live on.

Friends indeed, friends please heed,
Small deed, my creed.

My son, my seed,
I leave to you all that you need.

My legacy I cede,
My heart doth bleed.

My future, my life, oh God have I tried,
Oh God, I am unaware,
Oh God, I am blind.

Unrequited Love

I'm glad we had this time together,
I know in my heart my memories will last forever.

My vision of you is sealed in steel,
Your warmth and charm I can always feel.

Warmth so deep,
Beauty replete.

Eyes so beautiful puts lilacs to shame,
Skin so soft makes roses feel the same.

Our time together can't be measured in weeks or days,
Time is frozen things seem in a haze.

Our time was blissful,
Our time was divine,
Darling I'll miss you,
So glad you were mine.

Someone Homeless

Someone homeless sleeping there
Does anyone really care?
Why is life so unfair?

Out of work, and can't get a job,
What can I do? I don't want to rob.

When he was young he had dreams too,
Now they all seem untrue,
Any wonder he's feeling blue,
Not to me, I would be too,
How about you?

Summer Night

Summer night moon so bright,
Oh moon you are so beautiful tonight,
To walk by without looking just doesn't seem right.

The rain comes like a waterfall,
Gives strength to the pines to make them tall.

Oh how wonderful it would be to walk in the rain just you and me,
Oh sweetheart you make me feel so free,
Your blue eyes remind me of the deep sea.

Bluer than blue attracts my gaze,
You are such a beauty I am truly amazed.

Such beautiful blond hair I am so awe struck,
I keep thinking to myself what wonderful luck.

A peacock would feel very ashamed to walk by you,
He would turn tail, and run from your view.

Tonight was blissful,
Tonight was divine,
Tonight was tranquil,
So glad you are mine.

The Lonely Light the Lonely Night

Dark.

One lonely night,
One lone light,
Stood by himself.

Railroads were a bother with so much noise,
But oh how he missed them during the void,
When there was a void,
A sad void.

He missed his friend the sun only seen rarely,
Brother moon kept him company sometimes,
But he did not always call,
And so he wasn't such a good friend after all.

So jealous of the sun for his size, strength, and brilliance,
Pain of parting,
Eyes open,
Tears, and only a glimpse of his friend the sun.

Brief greeting, brief parting, and a momentary smile,
And then alone again in the dark.

The Lonely Ship

I sat on the side of the shore,
Wondering when I would do my next tour.

I fought in many battles,
I made my enemies cry,
I took no prisoners,
I never said die.

Through seas with typhoons,
Through torrents of rain,
I voyaged fearlessly,
I escaped unscathed.

The deckhands were sure,
The captain was brave,
And we made our name felt,
It made the enemy outraged.

And now that the war is over,
And now that the fighting is at an end,
I wish someone would visit me, or just be my friend.

Bring me flowers and at least remember my name,
Valiant soldiers fought beside me,
Surely that should bring some fame.

Oh little girl sit on my deck,
And I'll show you I'm more than a wreck.

I'll fire my cannons,
I'll make the gulls flee.

I'll tell you of the war,
You'll become part of me.

The Man Who Was Blind

I saw someone who was in a bind,
On closer inspection I saw that he was blind,
I gave him my hand, and asked do you mind?
He said no, and that I was kind.

Around construction we did walk,
I asked him his name to get him to talk,
He wasn't afraid, he didn't balk.

Helping him wasn't hard to do,
Being kind is easy, you can do it too.

Tonight

I wish you were here tonight,
To hold hands in the soft moonlight.

To gaze at the waters,
To lie on the shore,
Watching the ducks glide together,
Who could ever want more?

Monarch butterflies flying with ease,
As the larks sing their songs up in the trees.

To hold your body tight,
Be with me tonight.

Darling, your voice makes me quiver inside,
Gives me great pleasure I must confide.

Your laugh is enchanting,
Your eyes romanting,
Let's face it when I'm with you I'm panting.

I've never met someone with your great looks,
Not even the great heroines in classic books.

Outshine Juliet, put Shakespeare to shame,
I know in my heart you would inspire songs, and earn great fame,
Oh you are a special dame.

Your beauty could outshine the sun,
And I must confess when we aren't together the world feels empty,
I feel undone.

Tree

The tree grew proud and tall never expecting the axe to fall.

It was majestic and filled my gaze,
I could spend hours underneath lost in a daze,
It was home to squirrels,
And for young boys to play.

The bark was it's skin,
The leaves it's hair,
It surrounded him, protected him, but it was never enough.

When they chopped him down I grew afraid,
Especially when we looked at his freshly dug grave.

We read his lines two hundred years old,
An oak, a friend, whom I climbed, and story I've often told.

And now I am old, but you are not yet,
Here is a tale I hope you will not forget.

Youth is fleeting the bible says, but love lives on.

Grandson, objects collapse, the young grow old,
We must love each other, people must be told,
Love is everything,
Love cures all,
Cures the common cold.

Cures a broken heart,
Cures your fellow man,
Give it freely,
Give it often as you can.

What's It Going to Take

What's it going to take to change your faulty view?
That what you eat does not affect your health, or anything you do.

That eggs and cream, and that oh so tasty tart,
Never spells trouble for your quickly beating heart.

My father saw the doctor, and was told the bad news,
He would have to operate, and make the bomb defused.

Cut open his chest, and make his legs spaghetti,
Give his family nights of crying, and make his body messy.

And then comes time for the donation of blood to avoid getting AIDS,
And even that did not prepare him for the furious painful blaze.

And I felt so sad and even cried in the bathroom,
I was scared he almost died, and I prayed for him often.

I prayed for him to live,
I prayed for God to redeem him,
I pared for God to remind him.

And over time he recovered and became a different man,
And now he exercises as much as he can.

And eats a better diet,
And avoids grams of fat,
But often I wonder if he will ever go back.

So I tell you today don't even choose,
Don't wait till the doctor gives you awful news.

Live a simple life, have friends, and exercise often,
And you may yet be healthy,
There will be no need yet for an early coffin.

Who Am I?

Her eyes are emerald green,
Her face is ebony black,
Her true nature can't be seen,
She never looks us back.

Diligently we toiled,
Waiting for some result,
But we are often foiled,
And are left to molt.

What options are there left?
But to wait for her reply,
You have to be quite deft,
To look a computer in the eye.

Witness to Whiteness

I watched the hard compact balls of snow pass by me,
Moving like bullets from a gun.

The battle waged savagely on the grounds of SUNY Albany with
volleys and parries, attacks, and counter attacks.

Fighting with such ferocity at this time of night you would think you
were on the front lines of a world war.

Movement back and forth like stampeding cattle. With yelling and
shouts of joy, and then crushing defeat.

The thump sound of balls hitting their intended target,
And the softer sound of the ones off track.

I wonder how many of the participants are smiling.

I couldn't tell in the cold black darkness, but I could imagine a group
of so many imperfect smiles that it would give my orthodontist fits of
joy.

I was a witness to all of this when a geodesic mini moon nearly made
me unconscious.

I was saved by the thick glass windowpane and wind controlled-
door.

Then smiling I peered underneath the white mark, and gazed on in
eagerness at the ensuing battle.

Participating vicariously, I dance back and forth, while sitting in my
cold but comfortable wheelchair.

Parkland

I remember Parkland,
And Dublane too,
But so many people are forgetting,
And that's the awful truth.

Images on the news seem to be quickly out of mind,
The Pulse nightclub, Las Vegas, and children of Sandy Hook
Taken way before their time.

And all I hear is arm the teachers!
Guns don't kill people do!
But babies sometimes find weapons,
And that is also true.

So NRA I hear you, I know you want your guns,
But remember the lives of your mothers, fathers, brothers, sisters,
daughters, and sons.
You want to protect yourself in these troubled times,
But there are troubled people who kill without rhyme.

I wish I had a solution, a solution to solve it all,
But I am just a poet, so I will let the politicians make the call.

But still I wonder when looking for inspiration,
Will there ever be changes to the gun laws,
Or another mass shooting in our gun-filled nation?

Obsessions

Are obsessions ever good for us?
Do they ever make us strong?
Or do they just bring us to our knees?
Because we know that they are wrong.

My friend obsesses about his job,
But dwelling doesn't do a thing,
It just keeps him up at night,
And gives him endless grief.

Some obsess over women,
They can't get enough,
And yet even when satisfied feel empty,
Because they know it isn't love.

Some pine for unrequited love,
Some pursue lost dreams, and never give up.
Obsessions are like misplaced keys and wallets,
They can make life extremely tough.

But having a goal and taking small steps is a good place to start,
Just don't let your thoughts be your master,
Because they can become a new drug.

So keep dreaming and pursue what gives you joy,
Just remember to keep certain thoughts fleeting,
Obsessions can often make life feel wrong.

Powerless

Anthony Bourdain hung himself,
And Kate Spade too,
And I felt powerless,
Because I didn't know what to do.

I don't want to leave flowers,
My brother doesn't want to talk at all,
I try to raise the topic,
I try to discuss their fall.

Too often the desires of the heart,
Seem to win in the end,
It's just too easy to lose a loved one,
Or lose an important friend.

Depression, drugs, diets and desires or demands that we face,
Can often make us feel hopeless,
And sometimes feel disgraced.

A friend may call and ask if you would lend a hand,
Do you truly hear them?
Do you think that you can?

I'm not a professional,
I don't have the degrees,
But you have your humanity,
And that's worth a thousand framed trees.

So listen to your neighbor, your brother, or your wife,
Hear the words that are spoken,
Hear them when they cry.

And give advice if asked,
Or an intervention if there's need,
Because life often becomes better,
You can plant an important seed.

Give the number of a therapist that listens to what you say,

Tell the person that you're there for them,
And that suicide is not way.

Do You Know Brave?

Do you know brave?
I think I might,
I don't think it's me,
At least not every night.

I see it in the soldiers,
The FDNY,
The police when called to a scene,
And doctors, nurses, and EMT's when saving lives.

There are people coping with cancer,
And the loss of a home,
Children with a terrible illness,
And those who now live alone.

But here too at a bagel store,
Located on L.I. turnpike,
I think I see it also,
By everyday people living their lives.

I see it in the one-legged girl who talks about science, and laughs as if
nothing's wrong,
The 95 year-old World War Two veteran who reads his kindle and
stumbles along,
Both are friendly and going about their day,
You never hear any excuses coming their way.

The special needs woman or man who probably works harder than I
ever can.

They feel glad to be working,
Appreciate that they were given a chance,
Shows us that pre-judging is wrong,
And that we all can advance.

Too often we look on the wrong side of life,
While others live by example,
It's something we all should try.

163

So instead of staring or saying ill spoken words,
Learn from their examples,
Appreciate the diverse.

You can be brave too you don't always need to cry,
Face your troubles head on,
Are you ready to try?

Go Slow

The time clock's moving,
The payroll secretary disapproving,
And still I say, go slow.

Your date is glaring,
Her bed she won't be sharing,
And still I say, go slow.

The doctor is stewing,
Which procedure you should be doing,
And still I say, go slow.

The bride is blushing,
The groom is home and rushing,
And still I say, go slow.

The plane is starting,
Your flight is soon departing,
And still I say, go slow.

The kids have waited,
The principal is frustrated,
And still I say, go slow.

The mother has been pushing,
Her newborn needs a soothing,
And still I say, go slow.

Your life feels like it's moving,
The moments are yours for choosing,
And still I say, go slow.

Sunset at Steppingstone Park

It's 8:30 p.m. do you know where you heart it is?
I know where mine is,
It's here at the park with my mother and brother,
As we sit and watch the sun set.

The lights have just come on,
And in the distance the sun has gone to sleep,
And soon we will too.

But not yet,
Not yet.

There are still wisps of sun decorating the sky like cotton candy or
Kris Kringle's beard only orange not white or pink.

Tattered American flags line the dock fluttering in the wind like my
heart.
They are a reminder of a Memorial Day gone by,
Gone, but not forgotten.

Two planes fly in the distance in opposite directions,
And though I hear them I really can't tell what sound is which plane,
The sky grows in orange brilliance, and puts the LED lights to shame.

Sailboats and motorboats bob and bob,
And I try to ignore the mosquitoes as long as I can.

It was so hot today more like August than June.
I hid inside to escape and fell asleep by the air conditioner, and felt
more like a bear than a man.

But here at the dock tonight no AC is needed at all, but only a gentle
breeze.

We are witnesses to God's paintbrush,
And even the beautiful Asian women that walk past me like Gatzby's
green lights are forgotten for a while.

For beauty nature has no rival,
For it's sunsets there is no compare,
They are truly a marvel,
Steppingstone Park please wait for us,
Oh, how we all long to visit you and stare.

The Cataract

Father can you hear me?
I'm speaking to you with this rhyme,
Though you have passed away,
Your memories will live throughout time.

The teacher said you didn't write the poem,
But you protested and said, "I did!"
She looked at you and did not believe you,
But you knew in your heart that you didn't fib.

Her disbelief caused you to stop writing,
Her reluctance made you quit,
But I hope you realize she was misguided,
And I wish you were here to see *The Cataract* live.

You taught me to appreciate reading,
And corrected my writing many times,
But you never said I couldn't do something,
Those are gifts that will always be mine.

The cataract thunders like Niagara Falls,
The water flows beyond measure,
Though my father is not hear to read my books,
His lessons will live on, and that's something I'll always treasure.

Four Walls and Bars

Four walls and bars.
My name is Jose Feliz and I am a refugee,
It took us one month to get here,
But now I don't know if we'll ever be released.

Four walls and bars.
America is the home of the brave and land of the free,
Well, we swam across the Rio Grande, slept in a crowded safe house,
And spent hours in a truck that felt like hell,
That's sounds like courage don't you agree?

Four walls and bars.
The gangs wanted my daughter even though she is only ten,
The gangs wanted my son even though he is only nine,
The police threatened me, so we all said it was time.

Four walls and bars.
The president lives in a palace like the drug lords or so I am told,
While we have our cages, scraps of food, a small blanket,
And may never grow old.

Four walls and bars.
Now we are in America but I have no money and no idea where
my family is,
Even the animals live together,
In their eyes we are worth even less.

Four walls and bars.
The president thinks we are all MS-13,
But the criminals are why we are here,
Every day was unpredictable,
Every day we lived in fear.

Four walls and bars
I know you have your droughts because we have them too,
El Salvador means the savior,
But we learned that name isn't always true.

Four walls and bars.
We just want a chance to live our lives in peace,
We just want to be like you and live the American dream,
We just want a future and to be truly free,
Do you blame us?
You wouldn't if you spent one day in a cage like me.

Made in the USA
Middletown, DE
14 September 2022